1 On:

2018

ranch

JUSTICE FAILED

JUSTICE
FAILED

HOW "LEGAL ETHICS" KEPT ME
IN PRISON FOR 26 YEARS

ALTON LOGAN
with
BERL FALBAUM

COUNTERPOINT
BERKELEY, CALIFORNIA

JUSTICE FAILED

Library of Congress Cataloging-in-Publication Data
Names: Logan, Alton, 1953– author. | Falbaum, Berl, 1938– author.
Title: Justice failed : how "legal ethics" kept me in prison for 26 years /
   Alton Logan with Berl Falbaum.
Description: Berkeley, CA : Counterpoint Press, [2016]
Identifiers: LCCN 2017024767 | ISBN 9781619029927
Subjects: LCSH: Logan, Alton—Trials, litigation, etc. | Trials
   (Murder)—United States. | False imprisonment—United States—
Personal narratives. | Trials (False imprisonment)—United States. |
African American prisoners—United States—Biography. | Legal
ethics—United States. | Lawyers—Malpractice—United States.
Classification: LCC KF224.L55 L64 2016 | DDC 346.77303/34—dc23
LC record available at https://lccn.loc.gov/2017024767

Jacket designed by Bill Smith
Book designed by Domini Dragoone

COUNTERPOINT
2560 Ninth Street, Suite 318
Berkeley, CA 94710
www.counterpointpress.com

Printed in the United States of America
Distributed by Publishers Group West

10 9 8 7 6 5 4 3 2 1

To the memory of my mother, Mary E. Logan,
and to the hope that reforms are adopted in our justice system
so that the innocent are not executed nor languish
in prison for decades.

Contents

Introduction

by Berl Falbaum

Many of us have received a traffic ticket we believe we did not deserve. We drive away cursing, and vow to the heavens to take the fight to court.

If we lose the crusade for justice before a judge, we bemoan our fate and argue, to anyone within earshot, that the legal system is a disgrace.

Now, imagine the following: You sit in a small prison cell behind steel bars for twenty-six years convicted of a murder you did not commit. Then add this "minor" detail: Lawyers involved knew from the very beginning that you were innocent. How? A man they represented told them he committed the crime, but because of the standard of ethics in the law, the lawyers said they were obligated to keep their client's confession confidential.

The foregoing is not a fictitious scenario. It happened in 1982 to Alton Logan, of Chicago, and he tells his painful, excruciating story in this book, and he does so without anger or bitterness. He was—we have created a two-word term for what he experienced—"wrongly convicted" of murder. He faced the possibility of being sentenced to death.[1]

Instead of breaking their silence, what did the attorneys do? They drafted an affidavit stating that Alton Logan was innocent, locked the document in a strongbox, stored it under the bed of one of the lawyers, and did not speak out until their client died in November 2007. After they did, the wheels of justice turned, and all charges against Alton were dropped in September 2008.

We all know that life can, at times, be unbelievably cruel, forcing us to deal with financial calamities, catastrophic illnesses, or the premature deaths of loved ones.

Overall, most of us learn to endure, no matter how painful the ordeal because, ultimately, we attribute the circumstances to "fate" or, for those committed to religious principles, to "God's plan," and it is not our place to ask, "Why?"

We conclude that the tragedies we encountered were outside of our control and nothing could have been done to avoid them. We just have to accept that fact, and sometimes we need help to do so.

Being incarcerated, sentenced to death, or actually executed for a crime one did not commit, are entirely different matters because they result from avoidable human behavior, sometimes involving immoral, unethical, and even criminal actions.

Wrongful convictions—a catchall benign phrase that hardly reflects or fully describes the suffering of people who

---

1. Illinois abolished the death penalty in 2011.

encounter gross injustices from our legal system—stem from: incompetence, politics, ambition, corruption, deceit, indifference, peer pressure (in jury deliberations), bribery, perjury, and simple unintentional human error (for instance, mistaken identifications).

Acceptance of dire prison and death sentences, considering their root causes, should be, it seems to me, almost too much to bear emotionally and psychologically.

How does one sit in jail for decades or face execution knowing he or she is the victim of a poor defense, the skullduggery of a dishonest and overly ambitious prosecutor, or incompetent and even corrupt police? How do the convicted come to grips with continuous rejections of appeals sometimes based on obtuse legal technicalities? Even more frustrating, sometimes appeals courts offer no explanations for their decisions, which must be the most difficult result to accept. The "system" feels no obligation to give the wrongly convicted reasons why they will continue to languish in a prison or face death despite their innocence.

Under these circumstances, how is it possible for those wrongly accused, convicted, and sentenced to come to terms with their fate? How do they maintain the will to live knowing the steel doors of their cells may never be unlocked?

Or worse, how do they maintain sanity understanding that they face death despite the fact that they were guilty of nothing more than being caught up in a system where justice was blind?

These are the kinds of questions, among many, many others, that I posed to Alton who, while innocent, was sentenced to life imprisonment in 1983 and served twenty-six years behind bars for the fatal shooting of a security guard at a McDonald's in Chicago.

While exonerations have become more frequent with the development of DNA evidence,[2] Alton's case is unique—if that is the right word—because he was a victim of lawyer-client confidentiality, which, under a legal code of ethics, prohibits lawyers from divulging information received from clients. He was also the victim of blatant and reprehensible police misconduct and what he characterized as abhorrent abuses by prosecutors.

In Alton's case, two Cook County, Illinois assistant public defenders, Dale E. Coventry and William Jameson "Jamie" Kunz,[3] knew Alton was innocent. Their client, Andrew "Gino" Wilson, in custody for two unrelated murders of Chicago police officers, admitted to them that he killed the McDonald's security guard on January 11, 1982.

The attorneys stated in a March 2008 *60 Minutes* program that the requirement of lawyer-client confidentiality spelled out in the legal profession's code of ethics prohibited them from divulging any information that might hurt their client. Their

---

2. In 2016, addressing the frequency of exonerations while reporting on three exonerees, *60 Minutes* stated that wrongly convicted prisoners were being set free at a rate of ten a month.

3. Sadly, he died at the age of seventy-eight on November 20, 2016, about six months after the last time I talked with him.

duty, they emphasized, was to protect Wilson. They explained very comprehensively the importance of the affidavit, which they kept secret for more than two and a half decades.[4]

I interviewed both attorneys at great length in August–September 2015, and again in December 2015, and in the summer of 2016. From the beginning, I acknowledged that I did not agree with their decision. I wanted to be upfront and have them understand my position.

Kunz and Coventry were always candid, and did not refuse to answer any questions. I was impressed with their conviction to maintain the promise they made to their client. They repeated the obligation they had to Wilson numerous times. The two felt very strongly about the principle, and regretted deeply the price Alton paid for their unwavering decision to remain silent. Coventry, with whom I also talked several times in 2016 on the telephone, said in my last interview with him, that if I "hammered" him in the book, he

---

4. The affidavit was also signed by Marc Miller, an assistant public defender representing Edgar "Ace" Hope, Jr. who was with Wilson when he fired the fatal shotgun blast and who was charged with murder in the McDonald's case as well as the subsequent fatal shooting of a police officer. While I talked to Coventry and Kunz extensively, Miller, citing personal problems, said he would be unable to conduct any interviews with me. Andrea D. Lyon, an attorney in the Special Homicide Task Force Division of the Public Defender's Office, notarized the document. Lyon, dean of the Valparaiso University Law School when I spoke to her in 2015, told me it was her idea to prepare the affidavit and she drafted it. She stated Kunz and Coventry needed evidence that Wilson made the confession when he did. Admittedly disturbed by the circumstances, she was bound, she said, as were Kunz and Coventry, by the confidentiality requirement, particularly since she helped in the preparation of Wilson's defense. She said the three talked about the case many times, "but there was no way around it." Like Coventry and Kunz, she was forthright in interviews with me.

would understand. He stood up for his convictions, and was prepared to take criticism.

I said I admired him for that, and I commended Kunz as well for his openness.

The questions raised by the attorneys' decision are many: How did they live with the burden of knowing an innocent man was in prison, a man who could very well be free if they broke their silence? How did the attorneys raise families, take vacations, and engage even in the most mundane chores when in possession of information that could free an innocent man who was incarcerated for more than two and a half decades? To many, that is simply unfathomable.

I was very moved by the comment of a friend, Fred Keywell, a Michigan attorney, when we discussed the case. He listened intently and observed:

"I guess I could be disbarred [for violating lawyer-client privilege] but I would have to ask myself, 'Is it worth being a lawyer under these circumstances?'"

Kunz told me that he was "anguished" over the decision he felt he had to make. It was "wrenching," he said, and he talked frequently to his family about the case, adding, "I never second-guessed my decision. There is no question that I did the only thing I could do." Coventry similarly said he thought about the case many times over the years. He did not talk to anyone about it, not even his wife or other relatives.

If there was a bright side to the story, it was that Coventry showed commendable foresight in asking Wilson if he

(Coventry) could break his silence after Wilson died. Kunz said he was unaware that Wilson freed the attorneys from confidentiality after his death. The disturbing implication, however, is that posing the question to Wilson suggests that the two attorneys still would not have acted after Wilson's death except for the fact that he agreed to let them do so.

Alton might still have sat in prison after twenty-six years had Wilson not permitted the confession to be released after his death. Also, Wilson might have lived many more years. After all, he was only fifty-five when he died in prison on November 19, 2007.

Most important, Wilson's release was especially relevant and necessary for Alton because the U.S. Supreme Court has ruled that lawyer-client confidentiality survives death. In a 1998 case, *Swidler & Berlin v. United States*, Chief Justice William H. Rehnquist, writing for the 6–3 majority, stated:

> We think there are weighty reasons that counsel in favor of posthumous application. Knowing that the communications will remain confidential even after death encourages the client to communicate fully and frankly with counsel. Clients may be concerned about reputation, civil liability, or possible harm to friends or family. Posthumous disclosure of such communications may be as feared as disclosure during the client's lifetime.

Three justices disagreed. Justice Sandra Day O'Connor, writing the dissenting opinion, argued:

> Where the exoneration of an innocent criminal defendant or a compelling law enforcement interest is at stake, the harm of precluding critical evidence that is unavailable by any other means outweighs the potential disincentive to forthright communication.
>
> . . . The paramount value that our criminal justice system places on protecting an innocent defendant should outweigh a deceased client's interest in preserving confidences.

Alton was fortunate that Wilson approved releasing his confession after his death, and that he (Alton) did not have to rely on the law of the land as it relates to the lawyer-client confidentiality issue as decided by the Supreme Court.

In interviewing Coventry, *60 Minutes* correspondent Bob Simon observed, "I know a lot of people who would say, 'Hey, the guy's innocent, you've got to say so . . .'" To which Coventry replied: "Well, the vast majority of the public apparently believes that, but if you check with attorneys or ethics committees, or you know anybody who knows the rules of conduct for attorneys—it's very, very clear—it's not morally clear—but we're in a position where we have to maintain client confidentiality . . . It's just a requirement of the law. The system wouldn't work without it."

Coventry was acutely aware that Alton faced the possibility of a death sentence, and he was in court the day the jury announced its decision on Alton's penalty. The vote needed to be unanimous. It was 10–2 in favor of the state putting Alton to death; two votes saved Alton's life. Had Alton faced death, Coventry stated in interviews with me, he still would not have made the affidavit public. Instead, he would have sought a meeting with the governor of Illinois (at the time, James R. Thompson, a Republican) to ask him to save Alton's life.

What if the governor said, "No"? Would he have helped Alton Logan? Coventry said he and his colleagues had not discussed that possibility or other alternatives.

Kunz said, however, "I would have been prepared to lose my license. I was not going to let him [Alton Logan] be executed. It would have been an ethic[al] lapse . . . the execution . . . I couldn't allow that to happen."

What about Andrea Lyon, who drafted and notarized the affidavit? She said she would have acted to prevent Alton Logan's death, but did not know how. "It would have been more urgent, although this was urgent enough. Death would have been much, much worse . . . even though it's awful that Logan [was] in prison all [that] time for something he didn't do, there's something different between that and sanctioning his murder by the state by remaining silent."

She added that from a legal perspective the decision to keep the affidavit confidential was not a hard question. "It's not a comfortable question, but it's not a hard question."

Marc Miller, the assistant public defender representing Edgar Hope, was quoted in a Chicago newspaper story as stating, "We weren't going to let Logan go to the chair. He was sentenced to life, not death. And, reasoning from the premise that the attorney-client privilege is a cornerstone of American jurisprudence, the lawyers concluded that their duty was to honor it."

Addressing the difference between their decision to try to spare Alton's life by appealing to the governor if Alton had been sentenced to be executed but not for a sentence of life imprisonment, Kunz said, "I can't explain it. I don't know why that made a difference, but I know it did."

Alton disagreed, telling Simon on *60 Minutes:* "There is no difference between life in prison and a death penalty. None whatsoever. Both are a sentence of death." Asked if he counted the days and months, Alton responded, "I just counted the years."

Simon also asked the two attorneys if they considered leaking the information about Alton's innocence. Kunz responded that if he and/or Coventry had leaked Wilson's confession, "I lose more sleep if I put Andrew Wilson's neck in the noose"—the guilty man—than he would leaving an innocent man in prison.

Alton, on *60 Minutes*, said he could sympathize with the attorneys. However, he could not understand their silence. How could they not speak out when an innocent man was tried, convicted, and sent to prison for life when they knew he was innocent?[5]

Alton said the system is built to convict people and often misses the truth. "They are quick to convict. They are slow to correct their mistakes."

Kunz and Coventry acted, or actually didn't act, the attorneys said, not because of the Illinois code of conduct, which prevented them from speaking out, or because of possible disbarment if they had violated confidentiality. They kept silent, Kunz and Coventry said, because they had to keep their word.

Coventry continually stressed that the information being protected was the client's secret, not the lawyer's secret, and it is the duty of the lawyer to protect that secret.

The lawyers' decision has been described by many as unconscionable. The national legal code of conduct and the one in Illinois notwithstanding, their commitment to keep the vital information confidential seems to laypeople and some lawyers immoral.

Alton might very well have died in prison, a danger both Kunz and Coventry said they recognized. As Alton describes in these pages, he did suffer a heart problem requiring a stent implant in 2007, about a year before he was exonerated.

In a transcript of a public discussion on the subject of lawyer-client privilege sent to me by the American Bar As-

---

5. Months after the *60 Minutes* interview, when he learned about the code of ethics, Alton, to my amazement, actually expressed understanding for the attorneys.

sociation (ABA), a member of the audience, Professor Ronald Rotunda, of the Chapman University School of Law, made the point that the inviolability of client confidentiality was not as sacred as represented. He cited one exception, which permits lawyers to break confidentially if a fee is involved.

The reasoning behind this exception, as explained in the legal code of ethics, is that, "A lawyer entitled to a fee is permitted . . . to prove services rendered in an action to collect it. This aspect of the rule expresses the principle that the beneficiary of a fiduciary relationship may not exploit it to the detriment of the fiduciary."

In other words, in the legal community, lawyers are free to violate a pledge of confidentiality to a client in order to collect a fee, but not when an innocent person is facing execution or serving a life sentence in prison.

As we point out in the book, two states, Massachusetts and Alaska, permit lawyers to protect an innocent person from either prison or a death sentence, even at the cost of breaching lawyer-client confidentiality, by allowing them to provide vital information. The Massachusetts code states that a lawyer may reveal confidential information ". . . to prevent the wrongful execution or incarceration of another." The code permits, though it does not require, attorneys to reveal the relevant information. Massachusetts adopted its provision in 1998, and Alaska, which uses identical language, adopted the change in its code in 2009.

The exceptions in Massachusetts and Alaska prove justice

can be pursued without an uncompromising standard of lawyer-client privilege. Apparently, these two states have decided it can work, and Alton's misfortune, sadly, was that when he was charged, tried, and convicted he did not live in Massachusetts after 1998 or in Alaska after 2009.

Barbara C. Kamm, an assistant appellate defender who did outstanding work for Alton during his appeal process, made the point that if confidentiality between lawyer and client had not existed at the time Wilson acknowledged he killed the guard at McDonald's, Wilson might never have confessed. Her argument was that he may not have wanted to admit to the murder if he thought Coventry and Kunz would use the information. In effect, the secrecy provision in the code, in this case, actually contributed to Alton, ultimately, being released.

It is a valid distinction, but it should not be up to guilty parties to decide whether they will take the necessary actions to free the innocent. Wilson might even, again, have refused to release Coventry and Kunz from secrecy after his death, and Alton would have remained imprisoned for the rest of his life. He was only twenty-eight when sentenced.

Finally, Coventry and Kunz said that if they had come forward, the evidence probably would have been rejected in court because it was produced as a result of a violation of lawyer-client privilege. So, even the courts would have permitted an innocent man to die in prison. Coventry also said in my interview with him that prosecutors would not have accepted his information because it might have impaired their case against Edgar Hope, who was charged in the McDonald's shooting.

The legal system, including Kunz and Coventry, seems to agree that permitting the innocent to suffer because of lawyer-client confidentiality is "immoral," it is, nevertheless, "the law and legal." If that is true, it follows logically that the law and our legal system are immoral. That would suggest we need some changes because society is not served by an immoral legal system.

It is amoral, immoral, unconscionable, appalling for any society to *knowingly* allow an innocent person to rot in prison—regardless of the circumstances—without instituting means to free that individual. And, yes, it is unethical as well.

The bottom line question is: Would any lawyer in a case such as Alton's have remained silent had one of their loved ones sat in jail under the same circumstances?

Kunz said he could not answer because I had asked "a hypothetical question that was abstract."

Coventry said, spontaneously, "Of course, hell yes [he would have broken his silence] if it were my son, daughter or grandkids. But, I would recognize it would be a complete violation of my obligation."

Tempering his answer, he added he would withdraw from the case—recuse himself. When I responded that his withdrawal would not free his loved one, he said the question was hypothetical and he could not answer it definitively.

Lyon responded quickly, stating, "The answer can't be

any different, unfortunately. I wouldn't say it wouldn't feel worse," meaning she would have remained silent. Her response is very difficult to accept. Yes, she gets credit for consistency. Nevertheless, it is highly unlikely that she would let a son, daughter, or other loved ones sit in prison while innocent when she had the potential power to free them. In my interviews with her, she had a unique idea on how to possibly change the ethics code, perhaps the best solution offered to us, and it is discussed in Chapter 13, which deals with amending the ethical standard on this issue.

As to Coventry and Kunz, it is very hard to believe that they would permit a loved one to remain in prison under these circumstances. It is very doubtful any lawyer would let a loved one who is innocent remain in prison for even one year if they had information that might have them released. Coventry agreed that the question of a loved one's imprisonment while innocent was the most difficult question of all, and he could not answer it because, "I have never been in that position." Respectfully, I don't believe one has to be in that position to answer the question. Yes, my question was hypothetical. It was not abstract.

Though the attorneys and the legal system, overall, may think they are standing on principle, it is, after all, easy to pledge allegiance to an uncompromising code of ethics when there are no consequences.

I have been a journalist for more than fifty-five years, and that includes being a member of the adjunct journalism faculty at Detroit's Wayne State University for forty-five years. One of the courses I taught was ethics and when it came to discussing when, if ever, journalists should reveal news sources, most students, being young idealists, generally replied, "Never."

I would challenge them by presenting a variety of scenarios, and it was most telling how they changed their positions when life was endangered—especially that of a relative. That is the issue: Absolutism sounds principled when nothing is at stake; it is quite another matter when the results of absolutism cost someone his or her life.

I might point out that absolutism on a parallel media ethical issue claimed by journalists has frequently been rejected by the legal community. From the U.S. Supreme Court down, courts have not always recognized an absolute privilege for journalists in not revealing sources. Many a judge has charged reporters with contempt of court and jailed them for refusing to divulge sources. Courts have not accepted the argument that forcing reporters to do so had "a chilling effect" on sources cooperating with them, thereby hurting the public interest. The journalists' position is the same one lawyers use in their arguments that diluting the absolutism of lawyer-client privilege would make clients less likely to tell them all they need to know.

Interestingly, I discovered as I worked on this book, members of the legal community with whom I discussed Alton's ordeal generally agreed with the four lawyers involved. Harold J. Winston, assistant public defender and attorney supervisor in the Office of the Cook County Public Defender, a man with a keen mind and passion for justice who fought hard for Alton in the courts, also supported the lawyers. He even commended them creating the affidavit, and obtaining a release from Wilson that they could reveal his secret after his death.

Alton eventually shared that view. When I asked him how he could do that, he said, after reflecting on all the abuses committed by the police and prosecutors, the attorneys were the only ones "who followed the rules." However, he believes that "the rule" should be changed as he and I recommend in Chapter 13. How he can be so generous and understanding I will never be able to comprehend.

However, laypeople with whom I debated the issue condemned the lawyers. I do not remember any exceptions. Most were appalled.

In introducing the Alton Logan segment on *60 Minutes*, Simon said that the case cuts to the core of America's justice system. The same can be said about other miscarriages of justice that occur regularly.

Those miscarriages are many, and Alton was a victim of those as well. I'll just touch on one: prosecutorial and police misconduct. I discovered that unlike the uniqueness of Alton's case, prosecutorial and police misconduct has been described as rampant by many in the profession.

It happens often, and one would think that as innocent people are railroaded, and it is clear that they are innocent, someone would say: "Hey, hold it. This isn't right. This defendant is innocent." It is incomprehensible that those in the system, some with advanced degrees—prosecutors, judges, police, and other officials—(a) hide from the truth; (b) cannot see the truth; (c) distort the truth; or (d) do not want to see the truth, for whatever reason.

Why do these professionals stand idly by as lives are destroyed? Why doesn't anyone seem to care? Answers are not easy to come by. Some of the reasons include: Not wanting to rock the boat, fear of retribution, fear of losing a job or promotion, or fear of being labeled a whistleblower who, in our society, is usually ostracized instead of rewarded as he or she should be. The result: Innocent people go to prison for many years, and some go to their deaths.

The dishonesty of prosecutors is generally rooted in ambition—which Marc Antony, in Shakespeare's *Julius Caesar*, described as a "grievous fault."

A good record on winning convictions can lead to promotions, higher public office, salary increases, favorable media attention, attractive offers from private law firms, and longed-for respect for being a tough no-nonsense prosecutor.

What's more, district attorneys and their assistants know they face little likelihood of being held accountable. Why? Because they are immune from civil suits.

The immunity against civil action was defined in 1976 in *Imbler v. Pachtman*, a landmark U.S. Supreme Court decision. By a vote of 8–0 (with one justice not participating), the court ruled emphatically that prosecutors enjoy absolute immunity from civil suits.

In *Imbler*, which became the governing case on the issue of immunity for prosecutors, the court acknowledged that its ruling provides defendants with little recourse to obtain some kind of justice after suffering serious abuses at the hands of dishonest prosecutors. The court said:

"To be sure, this immunity does leave the genuinely wronged defendant without civil redress against a prosecutor whose malicious or dishonest action deprives him of liberty."

Pretty strong language. Understanding, sensitive and sincere. However, the court added:

"But the alternative of qualifying a prosecutor's immunity would disserve the broader public interest. It would prevent the vigorous and fearless performance of the prosecutor's duty that is essential to the proper function of the criminal justice system."

To buttress its decision, the court cited the eminent, oft-quoted U.S. Appeals Court Judge Learned Hand who, on the same subject, had stated:

"As is so often the case, the answer must be found in a balance between the evils inevitable in either alternative. In this instance, it has been thought in the end better to leave unredressed the wrongs done by dishonest officers than to subject those who try to do their duty to the constant dread of retaliation."

With all due respect to the justices and Judge Hand, they had it backwards. It does not serve the public interest to have innocent people executed or have them rot in prisons, all because of dishonest, immoral, and unethical behavior of prosecutors. It is faulty logic. If the threat of lawsuits tempers prosecutors' vigilance, so be it.

As a society, we have always believed that it is preferable to have a guilty person set free than an innocent one go to prison. We would be much better off by forcing prosecutors to abide by the highest standard of integrity and honesty, even if that were to lead to fewer convictions and a less ardent approach to win guilty verdicts.

Prosecutors who do their jobs honestly and abide by high moral and legal standards would have nothing to fear from the courts, even if they were sued. They may have to endure the inconvenience of lawsuits, but that inconvenience is certainly preferable to giving prosecutors immunity from any sanctions, no matter how despicable their tactics in the courtroom. Inconvenience is certainly preferable to ruining lives.

The *Imbler* decision also seems to negate a concept set more than 120 years ago in *Coffin v. United States* (1895) when the U.S. Supreme Court stated that it is better that five, ten, twenty, or one hundred guilty men go free than for one innocent man to be put to death.

The court stated: "The principle that there is a presumption of innocence in favor of the accused is the undoubted law, axiomatic and elementary, and its enforcement lies at the foundation of the administration of our criminal law."

Though the court was addressing the presumption of

innocence, it seems that this credo would apply to the issue of wrongful convictions as well. Wouldn't the public interest be better served by warning prosecutors that they face very serious sanctions if they violate accepted standards that lead to wrongful convictions, than the reverse, i.e. protect them from punishment for dishonest actions and have innocent people go to prison or be executed?

Protection of the innocent ought to be the priority and the U.S. Supreme Court should make that message clear in its decisions to all parties in the legal system whether they are prosecutors, police, or defense attorneys.

The sentiment that it is preferable to have a guilty person go free than have an innocent individual found guilty was also expressed by John Adams, the second president of the United States, when he was a defense attorney. In 1770, while addressing the court on behalf of a client, Adams stated:

"We are to look upon it as more beneficial, that many guilty persons should escape unpunished, than one innocent person should suffer. The reason is because it's of more importance to community, that innocence should be protected, than it is that guilt should be punished."

What is equally disturbing is that no one in the system even apologizes for these tragedies. They go on with their lives as if nothing had happened. When I write "no one," that is incorrect: there was one exception and it stands out because it was so unusual.

A. M. "Marty" Stroud III was the lead prosecutor in Shreveport, Louisiana in a case involving murder charges against Glenn Ford, who was found guilty and received the death penalty in November 1983. (Ford's tragic fate was decided only about six months after Alton was sentenced.) Some thirty years later—March 2014—Ford was exonerated; another man had committed the murder. At one point in his imprisonment, he came within a week of being executed.

In March 2015, Stroud, in an emotionally searing letter to *The Shreveport Times*, admitted fault in not considering other evidence and suspects.

"I was 33 years old, I was arrogant, judgmental, narcissistic and very full of myself. I was not interested in justice as I was in winning." He apologized to Ford, to the family of the victim, to the jury, and to the court.

In October 2015, Stroud appeared on *60 Minutes* and repeated how distraught and agonized he was by what he had done. Stroud said he almost "threw up" when he heard that Ford was innocent. Describing himself as a "coward," he said he was caught up in the "culture of winning."

Ford was also on the program. Asked if he accepted Stroud's apology, he replied curtly with one word, "No." That is hardly surprising for a man who spent thirty years in solitary confinement in a five-by-seven-foot cell in the Louisiana State Penitentiary also known as Angola Prison and the "Alcatraz of the South." Ford died of lung cancer in June 2015, only fifteen months after his release. He was sixty-five.

While Stroud was contrite, the acting district attorney of Caddo Parish, Louisiana, Dale Cox, who was also on the program, maintained that the system had not failed. Stroud had nothing to apologize for. Cox stated that getting out of jail after thirty years is "better than dying and it's better than being executed."

The reporter, Bill Whitaker asked him, "Isn't the law supposed to provide fairness?" Cox responded, "It is supposed to provide justice." He even opposed Ford receiving compensation from the state. Indeed, when released, all Ford received was a $20 gift card. Asked about showing some compassion, Cox said:

"I'm not in the compassion business, none of us as prosecutors or defense lawyers are in the compassion business. I think the ministry is in the compassion business. We're in the legal business. So to suggest that somehow what has happened to Glenn Ford is abhorrent, yes, it's unfair. But, it's not illegal, and it's not even immoral . . ."

Although Cox may represent the extreme, the system, nevertheless, is too concerned with "winning" and is driven by uncontrolled ambition. Regrettably, no one in power is prepared to speak up.

The Supreme Court has extended immunity to law enforcement agencies as well. In *Connick v. Thompson* (2011), the court overturned a $14 million judgment awarded by a jury in a lower court to a prisoner, John Thompson, who was innocent. He served eighteen years in prison, fourteen on death row. During that time, seven executions had been planned for him.

The majority opinion, which centered on whether the lead prosecutor properly trained his assistants, stated in part:

"The role of a prosecutor is to see that justice is done . . . By their own admission, the prosecutors who tried Thompson's armed robbery case failed to carry out the responsibility. But the only issue before us is whether [Harry] Connick, as the policymaker for the district attorney's office, was deliberately indifferent to the need to train the attorneys under his authority." The court ruled he was not.

The vote in the *Thompson* case was 5–4, thus the case may very well have been decided by ideology (the conservatives comprised the five votes) rather than on the merits of compensating the victim for prosecutorial actions that almost cost him his life.

The decision was widely criticized. The *Los Angeles Times* wrote, "The court got this one wrong," and Nina Totenberg, legal affairs correspondent for National Public Radio (NPR), said a "bitterly divided U.S. Supreme Court all but closed the door" to prosecutors being held liable for damages when prosecutors violate the law to deprive a person of a fair trial.

Professor Erwin Chemerinsky, dean of the University of California, Irvine School of Law, wrote in a 2014 op-ed article in *The New York Times*, "In recent years, the [Supreme] court has made it difficult, and often impossible, to hold police officers and the governments that employ them accountable for civil rights violations. That undermines the ability to deter illegal police behavior . . . When the police kill or injure innocent people, the victims rarely have recourse."

In referring to the *Thompson* case, Chemerinsky lamented that the court overturned the $14 million verdict. "The fact that its [New Orleans] prosecutor blatantly violated the Constitution was not enough to make the city liable."

The major point is: Life is sacred and the law should do all that is possible to protect it. Even wrongly sentencing the innocent to only one year robs them of their lives and, I might add, liberty and the pursuit of happiness.

I also could not find any comprehensive statistics on sanctions meted out to dishonest prosecutors. The experts agree that meaningful punishment is "rare." Occasionally, the courts will hold prosecutors accountable and bar associations may take some actions. Even when prosecutors were punished, it appears that they received what is usually described as "a slap on the wrist." The Center for Prosecutor Integrity (CPI), which reports that prosecutor misconduct "extends to the highest levels," adds that fewer than two percent of misconduct cases are subject to public sanctions. When sanctions are imposed, they are often slight, CPI stated.

How rampant is the problem of misconduct? The National Registry of Exonerations (NRE) stated on its website (as of May 2017) that there were 2,028 exonerations since 1989 when the NRE was founded and the first wrongly convicted prisoner was exonerated based on DNA evidence.[6] Of that number, 1,039 or 51 percent were attributed to what the NRE called "official misconduct," which includes misconduct by prosecutors and other officials.

In 2013, Alex Kozinski, chief judge of the United States Court of Appeals for the Ninth Circuit, lashed out at what he called an "epidemic" of prosecutorial misconduct, particularly relating to what is called the Brady rule,[7] which requires prosecutors to provide the defense with exculpatory evidence that could materially affect a verdict or sentence.

"There is an epidemic of Brady violations abroad in the land," said Judge Kozinski. "Only judges can put a stop to it." Unfortunately, they haven't, and much of the fault lies with the highest court in the land.

In a white paper, "An Epidemic of Prosecutor Misconduct" published in 2013, CPI quoted numerous experts, including prosecutors, on the subject, and they called the problem "rampant," "pervasive," "ingrained," and "common."

James A. Yates, a retired New York State Supreme Court justice, responding to a *New York Times* article on the (lack of) accountability for prosecutors, wrote in a letter to the editor in June 2016, "I can attest that more injustice is done by

---

6. The National Registry of Exonerations (NRE) is a project of the University of California Irvine Newkirk Center for Science and Society, the University of Michigan Law School, and the Michigan State University College of Law. Incidentally, NRE reports that the wrongly convicted are being exonerated at a rate of three a week.
7. The Brady rule was defined by the U.S. Supreme Court in *Brady v. Maryland* (1963).

prosecutors hiding material evidence than by any of the other numerous flaws in our criminal justice system."

It seems all too clear that we need a more responsive, sensitive, humane, and just legal system. Most important, the innocent people sitting behind bars deserve changes in the law, changes that might give them back the freedom that was unjustly taken from them.

I also believe that another reason we witness malfeasance in the justice system is because few are ever prosecuted for perjury—civil or criminal. I discovered this while helping Alton with this book, and while working on previous projects.

Through the years, I frequently discussed this with friends who are lawyers, and they did not tell me I was wrong in my conclusion.

Statistics on how many civil and criminal cases are prosecuted annually are hard to come by, although the legal community seems to agree that lying under oath is very prevalent. Yet, prosecution of perjury is rare.[8]

Obviously, like prosecutors and police personnel, people will lie, and do so blatantly since they face no prospects of any punishment. Thus, the oath "to tell the truth and nothing but the truth" is generally the first lie. In my research, I came across a story, perhaps apocryphal, in which a judge

---

8. One study I found reported that between October 2008 and September 2009, there were 184,000 felony charges and arrests but only 185 for perjury. A news story regarding perjury published in *The New York Times* in 1998 stated that of almost 50,000 felony cases only 87 involved perjury.

began his cases pounding the gavel and exclaiming, "Let the perjury begin."

In 2006, Oakland County, Michigan Circuit Court Judge Michael D. Warren, Jr. made the front page of *The Detroit News* when he announced he would begin holding people accountable for perjury. What laypeople would consider standard operating procedure in the courts was Page One news. In making his newsworthy announcement, Judge Warren said:

"There are very few judges who take it [perjury] seriously. That only encourages those people who have a predilection to break the law to continue to do so. People respond to sanctions . . ."

He added: "What we forget here is that perjury is not just an affront to the court, it has severe consequences for the party playing by the rules." One is tempted to respond with a facetious, "No kidding?"[9]

Justice demands we enact reforms. Regrettably, there is little motivation to improve the system, primarily because

---

9. I was curious what results Judge Warren experienced and interviewed him in 2015. He said he had pursued about twenty cases of perjury. As a result, perjury was committed less in his courtroom since the parties appearing before him knew he would hold them accountable. Usually, he said, the prosecutor declined to follow up on his proposed perjury cases, so he used his contempt of court power to charge individuals and assigned special independent prosecutors to investigate the case. Those found guilty faced ninety-three days in jail and a $7,500 fine. The major point: fewer people committed perjury before Judge Warren and that, of course, should be the key objective. Paul Walton, Oakland County's (Michigan) chief assistant prosecutor, told me that his office rarely prosecuted perjury for a variety of reasons, the principal ones being: the office is not an investigative unit and perjury charges require investigations; perjury is very difficult to prove; and juries are reluctant to hold people accountable because, "They expect everyone to lie a little bit in court."

there is no public pressure. Why isn't there any public interest? For a variety of reasons: the public has little sympathy for those charged with criminal offenses even after they are exonerated; only a small percentage of the public is ever involved in the legal system, civil or criminal, and, as a result, the public has no firsthand knowledge of abuses; the judicial branch of government is not subject to the same level of press attention the legislative and executive branches receive; and, overall, the media seem uninterested in the judicial process except when misconduct occurs in high-profile cases.

As Alton Logan's experience and the overall record of our system of *in*justice demonstrate, we need improvements, and we need them badly. Revamping three areas—the legal profession's code of conduct, holding people accountable for perjury, and punishing dishonest prosecutors and police officers would be a good place to start.

We must adopt changes. We owe it to Alton Logan and to the many—and no one disputes there are many—innocent people wasting away in prisons.[10]

In the following pages, Alton Logan tells his story in great

---

10. There are no definitive numbers available on how many people are wrongfully convicted each year. But Marvin Zalman, a professor of criminal justice at Wayne State University in Detroit who has studied and researched the subject extensively, states that there are one million felony convictions of all kinds in the U.S. annually. Of that number, he writes, a "plausible" projection is that one percent, a low estimate, or 10,000 are wrongfully convicted with 4,000 given prison sentences. The rest, 6,000, receive probation or "non-incarceration" sentences. Some estimates put the number of wrongfully convicted between two and three percent. Professor Zalman also has written in his studies that about three in 100 defendants sentenced to die are, in fact, innocent.

detail. He does so dispassionately and without self-pity. In discussing his ordeal, he raises important questions that we as a society need to face while adopting new policies that assure others are not caught up in the kind of legal quagmire that he suffered through.

The Affidavit

MARCH 17, 1982

I have obtained information through privileged sources that a man named Alton Logan (re. RD D-011952 M/B/28, 22 Aug. 53, IR# 282373) who was charged with the fatal shooting of Lloyd Wickliffe at on or about 11 Jan. 82 is in fact not responsible for that shooting that in fact another person was responsible.

Dale E. Coventry

SUBSCRIBED and SWORN TO before
me this 17th day of March 1982

Andrea D. Ley
NOTARY PUBLIC
My Commission Expires April 16, 1984

SUBSCRIBED and SWORN TO before
this 17th day of March 1982

Marc H. Miller

Wm J Kunz

Andrea D. Ley
Notary public
My Commission Expires April 16, 1984

P.J. Hominy
_V. J_

Preamble

Because four attorneys[11] signed the notarized forty-five-word affidavit on the previous page on March 17, 1982—roughly only one month after my arrest—and felt duty-bound to keep it secret, I served twenty-six years in prison, almost half of my life at the time, for a murder I didn't commit.

This is my story of the legal, ethical, and moral battle I fought and endured and how, with the help of a loving family, devoted friends, and dedicated attorneys, I survived.

—Alton Logan

---

11. There are five signatures at the bottom of the affidavit because an assistant public defender, Andrea D. Lyon, who notarized the document, did it twice.

JUSTICE FAILED

1.

Background

On February 7, 1982, when I was twenty-eight years old, I was arrested on Chicago's south side and charged with murder, attempted murder, and armed robbery, crimes I didn't commit. I was tried, found guilty in two trials, and served more than twenty-six years in prison—including about three and a half years in solitary confinement—before I took a breath as a free man again on September 4, 2008, at the age of fifty-five when the state declared in court that it was dropping all charges.

I had spent almost half of my life behind bars despite my protests throughout those many years to defense lawyers, prosecutors, judges, and juries that I was innocent.

I might still be in a cell if the real killer had not died in prison, thereby paving the way for me to have another shot at walking out of prison a free man.

I was also told that I was "fortunate" because when the facts came out the case was assigned to Cook County (Illinois) Circuit Court Judge James M. Schreier, described by all as an

3

honest and courageous jurist who worked hard to do the right thing. Other judges, I was advised, might just have affirmed my conviction, without examining the new evidence. Most wouldn't have wanted to challenge the system that put me behind bars for more than a quarter of a century.

I might start this story with the question I'm asked all the time: Am I angry or bitter? Well, I was angry for a long time and kept it inside of me. I'm still somewhat angry at some police officers, lawyers, and judges. Most of all, I am angry at the system, and I am very angry at one person, Richard Daley, who was Cook County state's attorney[12] when I was charged, tried, and convicted. I wanted an apology from him. I knew he wouldn't do it, and he didn't. I will write more about my feelings in this book.

Why did this happen to me? I will not try to explain the unexplainable or why God chose me for this fate. In this book, I will touch on the mistakes made and the gross inequities that are all too common in what we call our justice system in this country.

Of course, I'm not alone in having been imprisoned while innocent. I believe there are many—one is too many.

The good news is that more prisoners are being exonerated, primarily because of advances in technology and science, and particularly in the development of DNA evidence. My experience had a very unusual and, I might add, terrible twist.

---

12. Richard M. Daley served as Cook County state's attorney from 1981–89, and mayor of Chicago for six terms—22 years (1989–2011). His father, Richard J. Daley, was Chicago mayor for 21 years (1955–76).

That twist involved two attorneys who knew I was innocent because their client fatally shot the security guard at a McDonald's on Chicago's south side—for which I was convicted. They kept silent because they would not breach lawyer-client confidentiality. Two other attorneys, indirectly involved, also knew I didn't commit the murder or robberies. They too chose not to come forward because, like their colleagues, they wouldn't break the lawyers' code of ethics that demands adherence to lawyer-client privilege.

I was a victim of unfair imprisonment for other reasons as well. Police and prosecutors withheld crucial evidence from my defense lawyers, and the police intimidated witnesses. With their only interest in winning a conviction, police shamelessly lied about many facts, knowing all too well they wouldn't suffer any consequences or be held accountable. I strongly believe prosecutors knew all along of many, if not all, of the police's fraudulent actions in my case.

Before I discuss my ordeal, I thought I would begin this book by providing a brief summary of my background.

My family's roots were in the South, specifically in Jenkins, Kentucky, a coal mining town with a population of only about 5,000. My grandmother, Pauline Gordon, had six children: my mother, Mary E., her three sisters, Barbara, Matilda, and Zella, and two boys, Lind and Arthur. My grandmother never married; the man with whom she had the children lived nearby. He wasn't involved with the family.

I loved Jenkins. It was quiet with lots of farmland. I

still have warm memories of climbing "certain" trees in the backyard. I mention "certain" trees because there were several that my grandmother said were off limits. We could expect a beating if we disobeyed her. I made sure not to climb her favorite trees.

All six of her children moved from Jenkins eventually, seeking better opportunities in larger cities. There wasn't much work in Jenkins, nor much to do.

After graduation from high school, my mother first moved to Dayton, Ohio before going to Detroit to live with her godfather, Tom King, a former neighbor in Jenkins who, years earlier, had moved to the Motor City to join his brother.

I don't know how my mother met my father, Alton Logan, Jr. They married and I was born in Detroit on August 22, 1953. My parents and I moved to Chicago's south side to live with my father's mother, Melissa Logan, when I was about six months old. My family was Baptist and attended church every Sunday. My brother, Tony, two years younger than me, was born in Chicago on May 21, 1955.

My mother was sweet and caring. She was a God-fearing woman, very religious, and active in her church. She belonged to the church-sponsored Beautifying Club, which was dedicated to organizing events to improve the community. I was very close to her.

On September 15, 1955, my father, a steel mill worker, was shot to death in a robbery in an alley behind Pappys Liquors on S. Cottage Grove at East 47th Street on the south side of Chicago. He had just cashed his paycheck. The crime was never solved.

Since I lost my father at an early age—I was just two—I have no recollection of him. I was always told that he was a kindhearted man who liked to laugh and was very sociable. My Uncle Milan Cannon, my father's brother-in-law, was the closest thing I ever had to a father. He and his wife, Aunt Barbara, my mother's sister, spent a lot of time with me.

My mother was working long hours in a liquor store to pay the bills. Raising two boys by herself was too much for her so she sent Tony and me to live with my grandmother in Jenkins. My grandmother was very strict and, like my mother, very religious. She made me go to church four times a week. While I was in Jenkins, my mother had another child, Eugene, who was born November 19, 1960.

I attended elementary school in Jenkins, and it was a five-mile walk to school. Right from the start, I was always causing trouble. I had lots of problems with discipline, although I was never violent. My grandmother used "the switch" on me many times. It didn't help much. I didn't change my ways.

I was about eleven when the three of us—Tony, my grandmother, and me—moved back to Chicago because my grandmother was having more health problems as she aged. She needed help, and she wanted to be with her children—my mother and her sister, Barbara. I didn't mind moving back because we visited Chicago each summer anyway.

My family and friends called me "Lind" which is my

middle name, the name of my uncle. I acquired the nickname "Head" when I was in my early teens because I used my head in fights. That name stuck, and I was called "Head" on the streets and in prison.

I had lots of run-ins with teachers, yet made it through my sophomore year, the 10th grade, at the Christian Fenger Academy High School before I quit and looked for work. I really didn't quit school; I was asked to leave because I never attended classes. I looked for work, but I wasn't very successful at even finding odd jobs.

I started drinking when I was about fifteen, and drank into my adult life. I ultimately sought help and joined Alcoholics Anonymous (AA) when I was in prison in the late 1980s. Periodically, however, I fell off the wagon. I smoked pot. I never used hard drugs.

I was rambunctious, hotheaded, and had frequent encounters with the police. Once when I appeared before a judge— I don't even remember for what—the judge gave me a choice: either go to jail or sign up for the military. That, of course, was an easy decision for me. I chose the military and joined the Army.

I messed up again. After about nine months at Ft. Lewis, Washington, the Army threw me out because I was drinking and didn't follow orders. I received an undesirable discharge.

I returned home and found a job with the Neighborhood Youth Corps. I also started running in the streets, and got mixed up and made friends with the wrong people. We committed a bunch of robberies on the streets.

I had three crimes on my police record as an adult. In the early '70s, I was put on probation for stealing a car. After that, I was arrested and convicted for an attempted robbery at knifepoint in our neighborhood in front of a floral store. I was placed on probation for that as well.

I went to prison for the third crime:

In January 1974, I robbed an elderly white man of everything at knifepoint at 118th and Halsted. When I write "everything," I mean it; he was naked when I left. I also stuffed him, upside down, into a fifty-five-gallon garbage can. I thought that was funny when I did it. I stole his car as well. I was drinking when I committed this crime.

I was driving away when a cop named Jon Burge, in a scout car coming the other way to investigate the robbery, spotted the car I had stolen. Burge crossed the median and rammed into my car at 114th and South Halsted where the McDonald's—the site of the murder for which, while innocent, I would go to prison—would be built a few years later. I confessed to the robbery, and named others involved. I was convicted, and sentenced to three to nine years. I did five years from 1975–80 in four different prisons—Stateville, Pontiac, Joliet, and Sheridan. I was moved around quite a bit.

In one of those weird coincidences, Burge would be the command officer overseeing the McDonald's murder investigation. By that time he had moved up the ladder and was a lieutenant who headed a violent crime unit in a district known as Area 2. He had acquired a notorious reputation in the community for using any means to get confessions, including beating and torturing suspects.[13]

Burge also was in charge of a case, about a month after my arrest, which involved the fatal shootings of two police officers by Andrew "Gino" Wilson. That crime would prove extremely important to me because it provided vital evidence in my case that Burge and his men covered up.

I was released from prison on January 7, 1980. I realized the lifestyle that sent me to prison wasn't for me. I went job hunting, and I was hired at a book bindery. The job lasted only about a year before I was laid off because things were slow. I couldn't find another job, so I roamed the streets picking up cans, glass, and other stuff that I could sell. I collected anything that might get me a dollar. I was still living with my mother. I wanted to get out of the house. However, I failed in everything I tried to do.

Then *it* happened.

---

13. Burge was accused of torturing more than 200 suspects between 1972 and 1991. He was suspended from the police department in 1991 and fired in 1993 when the Chicago Police Department Review Board ruled he had used torture. Several investigations were conducted and in 2010, long after the statute of limitations had expired on torture and other alleged violations, Burge was convicted of perjury for lying about the use of torture by his crew. He was sentenced to four and a half years in prison, and served from January 2011 to October 2014 at the Federal Correctional Institute Butner Low near Butner, North Carolina. Burge was a veteran of the Vietnam War, and, according to Wikipedia, Ryan Cooper, reporting in *The Week* magazine, asserted that Burge probably learned to torture in Vietnam because his preferred technique was to use a hand-cranked generator, a common technique in Vietnam, where hand-cranked field telephones were widely available. Burge referred to the crank machine as his "nigger box."

2.

Arrest

I was doing pretty well staying out of trouble, but trouble found me. On the street, I heard about a robbery and fatal shooting on January 11, 1982, in a McDonald's at 11421 South Halsted at 114th Street, only four blocks from our house at 11618 South Morgan. Neighbors and friends were talking about it.

Two days after the shooting, on January 13, my mother told me that the cops had been at the house. "For what?" I asked. She said they wanted to question me about the McDonald's shooting in which one guy was killed and another wounded. I assured her, "I had nothing to do with that."

While the cops were in the house, they asked permission from my mother to search the premises. "Go right ahead," she said. "I don't have anything to hide." The officers looked around for about an hour. Of course, they didn't find anything.

The police left a business card and asked her to have me contact them. I called immediately. I wanted to get this out of the way. The cops came to the house, picked me up, and took me to the Burnside Police Precinct at 91st and Cottage Grove.

My mother followed us in her own car. At the station, three detectives questioned me for four to five hours before releasing me at about 2:30 in the morning. The detectives asked me to call them if I picked up any information about the murder in the neighborhood.

Here is what happened that night at McDonald's, which I learned later from media reports, court records, testimony at my trial, investigations by my attorneys, and most importantly, from a signed and notarized six-page affidavit written about seventeen years after my conviction in which Andrew "Gino" Wilson,[14] a black man, confessed to the crime.

I want to begin by correcting an error reported in much of the media: the shooting didn't result from an attempted robbery. At about 8:10 p.m. on January 11, 1982, two security guards, Lloyd M. Wickliffe, and Alvin Thompson, both black, were shot at the McDonald's.

Wickliffe, thirty-five, a Cook County Sheriff's Department sergeant working as a corrections officer who had been on the force for ten years, was killed, and Thompson, twenty-nine, a sheriff's deputy for nine years, was wounded. Both men were moonlighting as security guards.

Wilson stated in his affidavit that he and his partner, Edgar "Ace" Hope, Jr., also black, didn't intend to rob the restaurant. Wilson was in his car talking to a friend, Derrick

---

14. Wilson played a major role in bringing down Jon Burge. He filed a suit against Burge and other detectives, accusing them of torture. That suit prompted investigations, leading to the conviction of Burge on perjury charges and, ultimately, his imprisonment.

Martin, while Hope and another friend, Nadine "Nadia" Smart went inside to buy food.

Wilson noticed through the front window that Hope was arguing with a McDonald's employee behind the counter when the two armed security guards approached Hope and Smart. Wilson was concerned because there was a warrant out for Hope relating to robbery charges.

Wilson decided to go in, and he took with him a single barrel, sawed-off pump action shotgun. Hope was also armed with a handgun. As Wilson opened the door, one guard moved forward (toward Wilson), and Wilson raised the shotgun ordering the guard to "get back."

"At nearly the same time, I fired a single shot, striking him [Wickliffe] in the left chest," Wilson wrote in his affidavit. He stole the officer's .38 caliber revolver.

Meanwhile, Hope knocked Thompson to the floor, and stole a gun—a .357 magnum—from Thompson. Straddling the security officer, Hope pointed his revolver at Thompson's forehead. I had a lot of respect for Thompson's courage because I learned later from reports and testimony in court that while looking into the barrel of a gun, Thompson said to Hope, "Hey man, hey man, you guys don't have to come in here and hurt anyone. If all you want is money, go behind the counter and take whatever you want. But you don't have to hurt anybody. Whatever you do, please don't go back there and hurt any of these kids." He showed real guts.

Thompson later testified in court, "I looked up and saw

his finger. I saw his finger squeeze the trigger. I looked at his face and saw him smiling." Thompson closed his eyes and prayed. Just as Hope squeezed the trigger, Thompson turned his head to the right and moved his left arm across his face. Luckily, the bullet only hit Thompson's arm. Thompson rolled onto his stomach and pretended he was dead.

Hope thought he had killed the deputy. He learned later from news reports that Thompson survived. Wilson, Hope, and Smart quickly left the restaurant. Wilson pointed out the entire incident took three to five minutes.

From McDonald's, the four drove to the home of Donald G. White, one of their friends and a partner in crimes they committed. Hope talked freely about the shootings and showed off the guns. Wilson really liked the .38 because it was very small and had a sheriff's department insignia on it. He kept it with him all the time.

Wilson wrote in his affidavit that when he heard police arrested and charged me, "I put a gun to Derrick's head and threatened to blow his head off if he ever told what he knew." He said he also intended to warn Nadine Smart to keep her mouth shut, but he never saw her again.

Wilson admitted, in the affidavit, to feeling bad about my arrest, writing, "I never imagined Alton Logan would be convicted."

There are additional important facts in Wilson's affidavit that touch on other issues in my case. I will address them later in my story when, in 2008, Wilson's affidavit was discovered.

After the police interrogated me on January 13, I heard

nothing from them for weeks. About a month later, on February 7, 1982, my mother had gone to Detroit to help care for her godfather, Tom King, who was ill, and my brother, Tony, went to see a neighbor. When he didn't want to go, I told him, "Go ahead. I'm here for the night." Was I wrong!

Tony left the house between 11 and 11:30 p.m. He hadn't even crossed the street to the neighbor's house, he told me, when several scout cars screeched to a stop in front of him, and officers jumped out with pistols drawn. A couple of the cops who had been to the house a month earlier recognized Tony as my brother. The officers put Tony in handcuffs and locked them to the steering wheel in one of the scout cars. The cops asked Tony where I was, and he said I was in the house.

Would I open the door without resisting? Tony told me he answered, "He ain't got no reason not to." They didn't tell Tony why they were looking for me, but he knew it was about the murder at McDonald's. It had been the talk in the neighborhood. Tony also had heard about the shooting the night of the murder on a TV news program. After Tony left, I was watching television when the doorbell rang. My first thought was that it was Tony; that he had forgotten his house key. I opened the door and all I saw were pistols pointed at my head. There were about ten officers with their pistols drawn. They meant business.

"Don't move," the cops shouted. "You're under arrest for murder and attempted murder." I was being charged for the McDonald's fatal shooting. A warrant for "felony murder" had been signed by Cook County Circuit Court Judge Paul P. Preston.

After I put on my shoes and a jacket, I was taken, along with Tony, to the police station where I was interrogated like before.

At the station, Tony was handcuffed to a wall in a room used for interrogations. He was left like that for about five or six hours. At one point, detectives told him that I had confessed to the murder. Tony sneered, "that's bullshit because he ain't gonna confess to something he didn't do."

Tony was held overnight and released in the morning. No one offered to give him a ride, so he had to walk about fifteen miles to our home. He was warned that if he continued to complain, he would go to prison along with me.

Meanwhile, I kept yelling, "I don't know what you're talking about. This is all bullshit." I repeated over and over again, "Someone's lying about me. Someone's lying about me. I don't know who, and I don't know why."

I had lots of questions. One of them was: How did police get my name in the first place? I got my answer quickly. I learned that Nadine Smart, the woman who accompanied Hope into the McDonald's, pointed the finger at me. She was picked up by police after returning to the McDonald's while the cops were still on the scene. She stated that I was in the restaurant with them at the time of the shooting. Why would she do that when she knew that it was a lie? Various sources through the years speculated that she accused me for two reasons: (1) police were "sweating" her for information and (2) she gave them my name because she thought I was involved in robbing her mother's candy store. I think another reason she accused me was to protect Andrew Wilson since she was with him when he shot the security guard.

I had known Nadine Smart since she was an infant. She lived in the neighborhood. We knew the whole family. Tony, my younger brother, went to school with her, and as Tony said many times, "She had been a liar all her life." She and I weren't friends. We greeted each other if we met on the streets. That's all.

Detectives asked if I would agree to a lineup. I said, "Sure, put me in all the lineups you want. Line me up wherever you want. I ain't done nothing. If your witnesses say it's me, they're lying." I also waived my rights to a lawyer, stating, "I don't need a lawyer. Not for doing nothing."

A lineup was set up almost immediately, but not behind two-way glass. This was face-to-face, and the man I came to know as Alvin Thompson, who was wounded by Edgar Hope at McDonald's, identified me as the man who shot and killed Wickliffe. I didn't understand how he could make such an identification. I had never seen this man before. I had not been in the McDonald's.

No one even bothered to interrogate me; they had their minds made up that I was guilty. I was kept in a cell overnight, and the next day I participated in another lineup. This one was behind two-way glass so I couldn't see the people looking at me. After the lineup was finished, the cops let everyone go except me. I was told two more individuals identified me as the one who fired the shotgun. I answered angrily that the witnesses were lying. I had an alibi. I was with my mother and brother that night. I said that was easy to verify. All they had to do was ask them.

The two witnesses, who along with Thompson would play a major role in my conviction, were employees in the restaurant, Anthonette Dawson, eighteen, and Charles Trent, seventeen. Dawson was working behind the cash register, and Trent was the shift manager.

At trial, Jack P. Rimland, the attorney my mother hired to defend me, argued that the witnesses were, understandably, under severe stress and fearful since they were facing a man with a sawed-off shotgun who had just killed one man. Further, they only had a few seconds to look at both assailants.

In his opening statement, Rimland said eyewitnesses can be confused and mistaken as they were in my case. Many studies indicated witnesses frequently were wrong in their identifications.

"We are not here pounding our fists yelling that witnesses are going to be lying. We are saying that we believe that witnesses [can be] mistaken," Rimland said.

Corroborating and physical evidence was another matter, he said, and emphasized the state had none.

It is true that, even though Wilson wore glasses, there was a resemblance between the two of us. Our facial structures were similar. I thought and I still do that the three were pressured

I believed there were facial similarities between me and Andrew Wilson (right). He did wear glasses but it wasn't clear whether he wore them the night of the shooting.

by police to identify me, and that their identifications weren't "honest" mistakes as some believed.

For instance, Charles Trent, at my trial, described the shotgun from one end to the other. He knew every detail. He couldn't have done that unless someone coached him. He only had a few seconds to see the shotgun.

Anthonette Dawson was totally inconsistent in her testimony. She didn't tell detectives at the scene in McDonald's that she knew Hope and me; she didn't come forward with these "facts" until a month after the murder.

At the second trial she was almost charged with perjury because she added details she hadn't mentioned in the first trial. On the witness stand, she maintained she gave the same account in the first trial as she did in the second. That wasn't true.

Finally, Thompson, I believe, made an honest mistake at first. After all, here was a man who had a revolver pointed between his eyes only an inch away from his forehead. He had to be terrified. He could've made an error. Later, as we moved toward my trial, I believe, he was helped and pushed by police and prosecutors to identify me as the killer.

While terribly upset, I wasn't worried. After all, I had three witnesses who would swear that I was home at 8 p.m. when the shooting occurred. There was my mother, Mary, her friend, Rosetta Johnson, and my brother, Tony. The three would later testify, to no avail, that from the time they arrived home at about 5 p.m. until Rosetta Johnson left at 10 p.m., I never stepped out of the house. The shooting occurred at about 8:10 p.m. (I came home at about 4 p.m. after getting high on marijuana and alcohol with my cousin, John Edward Williams.)

When Tony returned home from the police station, he found the house had been turned upside down, ransacked. The police, looking for evidence and the shotgun used in the murder, almost destroyed our home. They even knocked doors off their hinges. Of course, the results of their search: nothing.

Tony called my mother in Detroit and she rushed back to Chicago immediately. He also notified several other relatives. My mother and her sister, Barbara, along with Tony, came to the station. They complained to the police about what had been done to the house and were told, "Sorry, nothing we can do about that. We did what we had to do." Weeks later, my mother even took photos of the house to the police. Her requests for compensation were rejected.

My mother brought me some clothes and cigarettes. She learned that I was being investigated for murder. The cops refused to let her see me. She couldn't believe what she heard. Murder? My son? Not possible. She also called my brother, Eugene, who was in the Army, stationed in Naples, Italy. She assured Eugene I was innocent, telling him that I was at home with her when the shooting took place. My mother kept Eugene informed, but he wasn't able to return home and visit me until August 1984, about one and a half years after my conviction. It was terribly frustrating for him.

I was transferred to the Cook County Jail and admitted to Abnormal Behavior Observation (ABO), a unit in which they housed suspects believed to be threats. ABO was used for prisoners that were guilty of crimes subject to the death penalty or were transferred to ABO from state institutions and faced life sentences. At the ABO, I received an orientation.

Officers unlocked a cell door, pushed me in and said that the other prisoner inside was my rappie.[15] It turned out to be Edgar Hope. He was charged in the McDonald's murder and for the fatal shooting of a police officer, which I will explain later. My rappie? I didn't know who this guy was; I didn't know him from Adam. I asked myself, "Who is this man?" I had no rappie.

---

15. Cohort, coconspirator.

We were in the same cell for two to three months, and we acted like men to each other. He didn't know me; I didn't know him. We felt each other out to see if we could trust each other. I didn't know that he had a part in the McDonald's shooting. I only assumed he did because the cops called him my "rappie." Since I was only charged with one crime, the McDonald's murder, that meant the cops believed he was my partner in that shooting.

Meanwhile, my mother hired Jack Rimland, using whatever meager financial resources she had. It wasn't easy for her or my family. My mother visited me as frequently as possible. Being a religious woman, she sought counsel from her pastor, and relatives and friends helped to boost her spirits.

Of course, as Rimland prepared me for trial, he told me that Hope was involved in the McDonald's incident. I also learned from Rimland that an accomplice of Hope's was the one who fired the fatal shot.

The morning after I was placed in the cell with Hope, I was taken to court where I was officially charged with murder, attempted murder, and two counts of armed robbery. I was before Cook County Chief Criminal Court Judge James M. Bailey who, at first, assigned the case to another judge. Then he changed his mind and decided to keep the case. I was informed that he was tough on crime and very pro–police and prosecutors. Regrettably, I discovered that all those who had warned me about him were right. He wouldn't set any bail.

Even though Hope and I were "getting along," I asked to be moved to another cell because I was tired of the games the cops were playing. I concluded they locked us up in the same cell hoping we would say something that would help them. I believed they put a snitch in a neighboring cell who was listening to what we were talking about.

In addition to the McDonald's double shooting, Wilson and Hope murdered three police officers in two different crimes that would overlap legally with my case.

On February 5, two days before I was arrested, Hope shot and killed a rookie cop, James E. Doyle, thirty-four, who was trying to arrest Hope on a Chicago Transit Authority (CTA) bus. Doyle, in his first week on the job, was in his scout car when a man reported that Hope, who had boarded a bus at East 79th and Lafayette, had robbed him. (I knew about the case because of massive coverage in the media.)

Doyle was shot in the head when he tried to remove Hope from the bus. Hope, using the .357 magnum he stole from Thompson at McDonald's, fired at Doyle's partner, Robert M. Mantia. He missed. Hope and Mantia exchanged gunfire and two passengers were wounded. Mantia and Hope ended up outside of the bus where Hope was shot in his side. He fell and dropped his gun. Mantia quickly cuffed Hope and confiscated from Hope the gun that belonged to Thompson.

Hope was taken to the Cook County Hospital for treatment. One of the wounded passengers, Cynthia Houston, seventeen, suffered a minor head wound, and the other passenger,

Kevin Paige, twenty-three, was released from the hospital after being treated for a hand wound. When I was shoved into the cell with Hope, I could tell he was still hurting from the gunshot wound.

On February 9, two days after my arrest, Andrew Wilson, twenty-nine, while with his brother, Jackie, twenty-one, shot and killed two police officers: William P. Fahey, Jr., thirty-four, a ten-year veteran of the department, and Richard J. O'Brien, thirty-three, who had been an officer for nine years. Both men were assigned to the Gang Crimes Enforcement Division and, tragically, were killed just hours after attending the funeral for Officer Doyle.

The murders took place at about 2 a.m. during a routine traffic stop at 81st Street and Morgan. It wasn't clear why the cops stopped the Wilsons. Arguments ensued, leading to the murders by Andrew Wilson, who stole the officers' guns before escaping with his brother.

Jackie Wilson was wanted for a parole violation and Andrew Wilson for a parole violation and bond forfeiture. Both had committed a burglary only hours before being stopped by Fahey and O'Brien.

The killing of four police officers (a sheriff's deputy in the McDonald's and three Chicago officers) and the wounding of a fifth (Thompson) in just one month angered Burge and the police generally, and also increased pressure on them to solve the murders.

An officer in the Fraternal Order of Police, William Nolan, was quoted in *The New York Times* as stating, "There is no respect out there for the man in blue. When policemen in full uniform are getting shot in broad daylight, the uniform means nothing!" The union offered a $10,000 reward for information leading to an arrest in the shootings of Fahey and O'Brien, and Chicago Mayor Jane M. Byrne added another $50,000 reward.

Burge and his men went into overdrive in violating the rights of suspects and people questioned. They became even more unrelenting and brutal than usual, and were devoted to only one principle in arresting suspects: the ends justified the means.

The community was outraged by the police rampage and racism. The city received hundreds of complaints about police brutality and civil rights violations. The civil rights leader, Rev. Jesse Jackson, of Chicago, compared the police campaign to a "military occupation." One detective described the search for the cop killers as a military operation, adding: "I don't know what Kristallnacht[16] was like, but this was probably close."

Responding to tips from the community, police, armed with a search warrant, on February 13 raided Willie's Beauty Shop at 1440 W. 115th Street, owned by Andrew Wilson's aunt. Police Detective Joseph Gorman said police found a sawed-off shotgun on a heater in a closet. Also discovered in the beauty shop were the revolvers belonging to Fahey and O'Brien.

A ballistics test conducted on the shotgun the same day

---

16. Kristallnacht (the Night of Broken Glass) was a pogrom conducted in Nazi Germany and Austria November 9–10, 1938. Thousands of Jewish homes, businesses, synagogues, hospitals, and other institutions were vandalized and destroyed. About 100 Jews were murdered and some 30,000 Jewish men were arrested and incarcerated.

it was found and just six days after my arrest proved that a cartridge shell recovered at the McDonald's murder scene had been fired from the shotgun. The ballistics report stated:

FROM: JOSEPH R. CELOVSKY, FIREARM EXAMINER

TO: DIRECTOR, MARSHALL CONSIDINE, CRIME
LABORATORY DIVISION

SUBJECT: SHELL RECOVERED AT SCENE

On 13 February 1982, a 12 gauge J.C. Higgins sawed-off shotgun recovered at 1440 W. 115th during investigation of Fahey and O'Brien, the undersigned . . . identified the weapon . . . as firing the evidence discharged shot shell . . . Identification was verified by technician Richard W. Chenow and *Lt. Burge, Area 2, Violent Crime, was notified as [sic] 1750 hours*.[17]

If Burge, his detectives, and prosecutors had followed up on that ballistics report, I might not even have been tried.

Police, with Burge leading the way, arrested Andrew Wilson the next day at 5:15 a.m. on February 14, Valentine's Day, in a closet at an apartment at 5301 W. Jackson on the west side of Chicago and across town from where I lived. Immediately, police should have questioned Andrew Wilson

---

17. Emphasis added.

about the shotgun and confronted him with the fact that the shell found at McDonald's matched his weapon.

Acting on another tip from the community, police arrested Jackie Wilson at 5157 S. Prairie, on Chicago's south side, about three hours after Andrew Wilson's capture. Reports were that the Wilsons were stealing weapons from police officers and burglarizing homes for more guns because the two planned to break Hope out of the hospital where he was recuperating from the gunshot wound. Why? Because Hope had contacted the Wilson brothers and warned them that unless he was freed, he would talk about all the crimes they had committed.

(After I was transferred to the Pontiac Correctional Center in Pontiac, Illinois, I ran into Andrew Wilson in the building that housed our cells in 1995, about twelve years after my conviction. I walked up to him and asked, "Why don't you come clean about my innocence in the McDonald's murder?" He just giggled and that's when I knew he committed the crime. I don't remember him saying anything back to me. He just turned and walked away.)

If hiding physical evidence was not enough, police interrogated Donald White, to whose home Andrew Wilson and Hope went after the McDonald's shootings, and White readily acknowledged that he knew Andrew Wilson had murdered Wickliffe in the McDonald's. That information was hidden as well.

In addition, as we were to find out, all the notes of my

interrogations, and explanations of why I was a suspect at all, were missing from police files. They were never found.

It was in this politically charged atmosphere that I waited in a Cook County Jail cell for what would be the first of two trials. It was very clear to me the cops and prosecutors were going to frame me. Everything pointed in that direction.

I could never have imagined such a scenario, let alone one in which two lawyers for Andrew Wilson, Dale E. Coventry and William Jameson "Jamie" Kunz; one for Hope, Marc A. Miller; and another lawyer indirectly involved, Andrea D. Lyon, knew I didn't kill Wickliffe but kept silent. I would learn about their reasoning two and a half decades later.

3.

Creating the Affidavit

In March 1982, about a month after my arrest, while I was sharing a cell with Edgar Hope, he did something that would ultimately lead to my exoneration.

Without my knowledge, Hope, according to court records, instructed his lawyer, Marc Miller, an assistant public defender, to inform my lawyer, Jack Rimland, that I was innocent. Hope gave Miller an "unequivocal order," to talk to Rimland, adding that it was Andrew Wilson who killed Wickliffe in McDonald's.

Hope told Miller that he didn't know me, that he committed all his crimes with Wilson who was his right-hand man. He said Miller could check in the "hood" on the relationship between him and Wilson, adding, "I only work with Wilson."

Again, I didn't know that Hope had done that; he never mentioned that he would try to help me. To this day, I don't know why he did it. Some speculated that Hope didn't want to leave any doubt about the fact that he "worked" with no one but Wilson, that he was proud about that relationship. Whatever the case, I was sure glad he did what he did though I wish it hadn't taken twenty-six years to undo my conviction.

Miller approached Rimland, saying something along these lines: "You represent an innocent man, and if I can help you in any way, I will, in any way but one." Miller meant he wouldn't jeopardize his client. Rimland asked Miller if he could interview Hope. Miller responded that he couldn't allow him to do so.[18]

As a matter of fact, once when Hope saw Rimland meeting with me in jail, he suggested to Rimland, "When you get through, there's something I'd like to tell you." Rimland suspected that Hope wanted to talk about the McDonald's shooting. Rimland tried to speak with Hope, but Miller wouldn't let him.

Miller took another step: He called Dale Coventry and Jamie Kunz, assistant public defenders who were representing Wilson in the murders of the two police officers, Fahey and O'Brien.[19]

---

18. Rimland told Berl in April 2017 that Miller never contacted him about my innocence. However, after the Kunz–Coventry affidavit was discovered, Miller filed affidavits and testified in court in 2008 that he told Rimland about Hope insisting that I was innocent. Rimland said he had absolutely no idea why Miller made those statements. Indeed, Rimland said that Miller maintained that if he talked to him he would be violating lawyer-client privilege. Miller, however, did call Coventry. So why would he refuse to talk to my lawyer about Hope's claim that I was innocent, but not Coventry, who represented Wilson? As Berl wrote in his introduction, he was unable to interview Miller.

19. As a matter of policy, the Cook County Public Defender's Office always assigned two lawyers to clients charged with capital offenses.

In his call to Kunz and Coventry, Miller said, "You think your life's difficult now? My understanding is that your client, Andrew Wilson, is the shooter in the McDonald's murder."

Regarding the call from Miller, Coventry told Berl:

We said, "Oh, shit." Our guy was charged with killing two police officers and you worry about mitigation and aggravation. Aggravation would clearly be a problem when he was charged with homicide in another case. We didn't think we could beat the death penalty in our case, but we didn't want it to be any worse than it was. We also didn't want to represent him in a second death penalty case.

So we wanted to find out and went to the [Cook County] jail, sat him down in a lounge and we asked him that we heard he and Hope were involved in the McDonald's killing. He was hunched over a little bit, and he said "Yeah." We asked him, "With a shotgun?" and he said, "Yeah." We knew he might be involved because he was Hope's partner and this might have been another one of their robberies. There was no remorse. He said it happened like a bunch of other stuff that happened. He said it very matter-of-factly.

Obviously, this is not information beneficial to him [our client] at all. We needed to know this information, but we didn't want to pursue it because it was not our case. We couldn't talk about it because of lawyer-client privilege, and we wouldn't talk about it because it would screw up his case.

Our interest was just to try and diminish the case that was already before us. We had this information, but we didn't know what to do with it. It was obviously privileged and we couldn't tell anyone about it. On the other hand, there was an innocent guy charged with this murder. So we discussed it and concluded that the least we would do was to memorialize it to indicate that we had this information. We couldn't just come out with the information at a later date because we would be asked why we never said anything earlier.

But if we memorialized the information we would have a dated, formalized, signed and also ambiguous document. We had a statement which said that Alton Logan was, in fact, not guilty of killing this guy but another guy who gave us privileged information was responsible for the death.

It was Andrea D. Lyon, another assistant public defender, who told Berl that she recommended drafting an affidavit so that if Coventry and Kunz were ever to reveal the truth, it wouldn't look like they made up the story. Under the circumstances—she was a part of the defense team helping Coventry and Kunz with motions and the investigation—she felt compelled to remain silent as well.

Coventry continued: "We did not know . . . what we would

do with that [the affidavit]. We knew that if Alton Logan were to get the death penalty, we would do something because while we kept our mouth shut, we could not go that far."

Faced with what the lawyers considered serious ethical issues, on March 17, 1982, they drafted the affidavit reproduced at the beginning of the book. It was signed by Coventry, Kunz, Miller, and Lyon, who notarized it. The four didn't make any copies.

Coventry said he purposely didn't have Wilson sign the affidavit, stating: "I didn't want it signed by him because I didn't know what kind of court order I might be given in the future to turn over the document."

Although Wilson's name isn't even mentioned in the affidavit, Kunz said in interviews, "It's pretty clear who we are talking about. 'Information from privileged sources' means somebody told us and that somebody can only be a client."

Addressing the moral and ethical dilemma, Kunz said, "It was sort of like playing an ethical striptease. It was a risky thing to do. If the affidavit had fallen into the wrong hands, it would get people in trouble, and any hands but ours would be the wrong hands. Even our mothers."

The major objective, Kunz said, was, "to make a time-stamped declaration against a subsequent claim that 'you guys are making it up now.'"

Coventry took the issue a step further, asking Wilson if he could divulge the confession after Wilson died.

"I had developed a very good relationship with him,"

Coventry said. "I try to do that with most of my clients. Many do not trust the system, and I tried to make sure he trusted what I told him. I established a trusting relationship with him that allowed me to ask him what I could do with the information I had. The implied question was, 'Could I use the information when he died?'

"I asked the question because he might get the death penalty for killing two cops. Another cop also had been killed, as well as the security guard at McDonald's—all within about a month. So the police felt like there was a war against them."

Wilson knew, Coventry said, why he posed the question, and he gave Coventry permission to talk when he died. Coventry stressed that Wilson's permission to allow him to break his silence after his (Wilson's) death was oral. Jamie Kunz, Coventry said, didn't know that Wilson released the two from confidentiality after he died.

"I keep things to myself," Coventry said. "I did not tell anyone about the document or the release after Wilson's death. Had I said that, it would have been a violation of his privilege."

Kunz acknowledged that Coventry didn't reveal that Wilson released the attorneys from confidentiality after his death.

Stating he would have broken his silence when Wilson died, Kunz added,

> I should point out that I did not even know that Andrew
> Wilson had agreed to let us talk after he died. I learned
> of his death during a phone call to Harold Winston

[of the Cook County Public Defender's Office, who would become the lead lawyer after my second trial]. My reaction, "Good." I discovered then that Wilson had apparently told Coventry, "When I die, you can talk." But Coventry didn't tell me. Maybe Coventry wanted to keep this secret because if it became known that Wilson released us from our commitment, someone would have killed Wilson in prison so we would be allowed to talk.

Expanding on his thoughts, Kunz added:

I talked to a very well-known, respected defense attorney who became a well-known judge. I asked him if there was something we could do, and he said, "No." I even asked him that if Alton Logan were sentenced to death, if we could have a group of lawyers ask the governor not to execute Alton Logan because he's innocent, and I was told, "No, we can't even do that."

The reasoning was that if you break your promise, you are inviting a reexamination of the case and inviting them to indict your client. I was told I couldn't even say, "You got the wrong guy" because I would have done something to put my client's neck in the noose.

Kunz acknowledged that "over the years, I talked to many people when the subject of innocent people going to jail came up. I didn't mention any names, but I would say, 'I know a guy and here's how I know.'" Kunz would describe my dilemma, again, without identifying me.

Kunz said he wasn't trying to abide by any code of ethics. "I was going by my personal commitment to my client. I was going by my own personal gut feeling that when your client tells you something, you keep your mouth shut.

"I kept the confidence not because of any code of conduct. I didn't even know what the code was in Illinois. I didn't say anything because I gave my client my word."

Nor, Kunz said, was he worried about disbarment if he broke his silence.

> That did not occur to me. I did not think about that at all. I was keeping a promise I had made to my client. I did think about possible lawsuits by Andrew Wilson's survivors. But I wasn't too worried about hurting his reputation [he was charged with two murders of police officers.] Also, his family stayed away from the case. We couldn't even get anyone to come to speak on his behalf when the death penalty was being considered.

Both Coventry and Kunz said that even if they had provided the evidence, prosecutors wouldn't have acted on it for fear of jeopardizing their case against Hope. The defense would have argued that if I was the "wrong guy," then it's sure possible that Hope was innocent as well. The prosecutors would never have taken that risk, they said.

Asked if he ever considered that I might die in prison, Coventry said:

> Yes, of course, I did. That question suggests an attitude. I am not criticizing that. But, the attitude is that the system is legitimate. That there is such a thing as justice, that the laws are followed. None of that stuff is true. Even the appellate court system exists to affirm what was done at the trial level.
>
> They would lose that case. They would rather convict Alton Logan than do the right thing. I am absolutely convinced they—the police and the prosecutors—knew they had an innocent guy.
>
> Prosecuting an innocent guy is not a problem. They wanted to prosecute Alton Logan because they got their witnesses to ID Edgar Hope. Once they got that they couldn't have their witnesses change their ID of Logan. They were the same witnesses. They would have said, "You are wrong about that guy, but right about this one?"
>
> What's more, in the real world of prosecution, the information would not be believed. Prosecutors are notoriously averse to admitting they are wrong. Going public would not save anyone. That assumes integrity on the part of police and prosecutors which just isn't there. Especially, if it involved someone I had an interest in, I wouldn't be credited.

The reason we made an affidavit was to counter the typical prosecutor's response, "You are making that up." Same logic as rejecting alibi witnesses, or even evidence the accused was in a lockup somewhere. Defense evidence is rejected out of hand by prosecutors, most judges, and frequently by jurors.

In Logan's case, the saying that "anyone can convict a guilty guy, but it takes a great lawyer to convict the innocent" was thought to be a good joke by prosecutors.

Coventry also pointed out, the Massachusetts code,[20] which permits lawyers to breach confidentiality if it may lead to the exoneration of an innocent person, was adopted in 1998, some sixteen years after the McDonald's murder.

Finally, Berl asked Coventry why he didn't ask Wilson to release him from confidentiality while he (Wilson) was still alive. Coventry replied that would have put Wilson "in jeopardy." Coventry explained:

My job is to defend him (Wilson) and to do what is in his best interests. His best interests were not to face an additional criminal charge . . . if he had made an admission, he would be facing another death penalty case. I would never have done it [ask him to release me from my commitment to secrecy]. I was trying

---

20. As Berl discusses in his introduction, Alaska adopted a similar provision in 2009.

to protect him. He was my concern. He would have been subject to another death penalty [if he released me from confidentiality].

I wouldn't let him do it. When I am defending somebody, they don't know the rules and ramifications of the law. I understood them considerably more . . . so that was not going to happen. We wanted to avoid getting the death penalty. In the end, we successfully avoided the death penalty [for the murder of police officers Fahey and O'Brien].

I understand Coventry's position, but it also implies that it was not all about lawyer-client confidentiality. It was also about protecting Wilson from another murder charge. Coventry is basically saying that while he was bound to keep his client's secret under the ethics code, he also didn't want to be released from that obligation because Wilson would face another murder charge, a charge that could've gotten him another death sentence. That was another reason Coventry didn't want to ask Wilson to permit him to talk while he (Wilson) was still alive.

Sure, even the guilty deserve the best defense possible, but defending the guilty at the expense of the innocent is another matter. That should be unacceptable.

So, Coventry locked the affidavit in a fireproof strongbox, and kept it under his bed. While I slept on a prison bunk in a cell for twenty-six years, Coventry was sleeping above a box whose contents could have set me free and spared me years in hell.

4.

First Trial, 1983

Almost exactly a year after my arrest, my case finally came to court. I had been caged in jail for a year, and I was innocent of any wrongdoing. I committed no crimes, none. Little did I know then that I would spend another twenty-five years—a quarter of a century—behind bars. That would've been incomprehensible to me.

I had been unable to convince the police and prosecutors of my innocence. Now, my hope was that I could persuade a jury that I was at home sleeping when the murder was committed, and, as I have already written, I had three witnesses—my mother, Mary, her friend, Rosetta Johnson, and my brother, Tony, to prove it.

Our defense rested entirely on my alibi witnesses—three of them—and the state's case hinged on three eyewitnesses. There was no other evidence—no fingerprints, DNA, or any other physical evidence whatsoever.

Throughout the year, I continually reassured my lawyer, Jack Rimland, "I can't tell you anything about the crime. I know nothing about it."

Of course, I was very angry. I made sure not to show it. I hid my emotions and I can't even describe my feelings. As time passed, I became less angry and more thoughtful. I worked on listening more. Maybe I would hear something that would help me.

Most important was the support of my mother, my brother, Tony, my aunt, Barbara Gordon Cannon, and my cousin, Gloria Williams, daughter of my mother's sister Matilda, all of whom attended the trial every day. They were very strong and that helped me. My mother assured me, "The truth will come out one day." Not only was the trial hard on my mother, she also was suffering from a very serious case of diabetes. It was devastating for my mother to hear that her son was accused of murder when she knew he didn't do it.

Hope and I were tried together. This wasn't our choice or a matter of strategy. We wanted separate trials. The judge, however, denied our motion because, apparently, it was more convenient for him to have the cases heard at the same time since we were both accused of the same crime.

In his opening statement, my attorney stressed: "Alton Logan does not know Mr. Hope. He does not wish, under any circumstances, to ever have any further contact with Mr. Hope after this case is over with, and he does not wish to be seated in this courtroom with Mr. Hope. [But] that is not his choice."

One major piece of evidence was the sawed-off shotgun, which was discovered in the beauty shop owned by Andrew Wilson's aunt and matched to the empty shell found in McDonald's.

Judge Bailey, described as being very pro-prosecution, refused to allow that evidence to be admitted. That evidence alone should have freed me.

Jack Rimland had the following contentious exchange with the judge on that issue:

Judge: I can't see the relevancy [of admitting the shotgun]. I don't see ballistically [how] you can tie up that shotgun. Can you ballistically tie up the shotgun? [*The answer to that question, of course, was that we could and the ballistics experts did.*]

Rimland: Judge, here we are talking about a murder weapon that the state, through their criminalistics investigation, shows that this is the same weapon that was used. Now, it is not discovered in the possession of my client [me]. It is discovered in the possession of other people. We are excluding evidence that is favorable to my client.

The judge didn't relent, and Rimland moved for a mistrial, a motion that the judge denied.

It was disheartening and devastating to say the least. The judge also denied other evidence to be introduced that would have helped me. For instance, he refused to let us show photos that would have revealed that Andrew Wilson and I had facial similarities. That would have helped explain the mistakes made by the witnesses.

What I was hearing was very troubling. I couldn't believe the reaction of the jurors. As witnesses testified, I looked at the faces of the jurors and what I saw worried me. At times, I thought they were undecided; at other times they seemed to accept the testimony that I fired the shotgun.

The trial lasted four days. My fate—whether I would go free, be executed, or spend the rest of my life in prison—would now be decided by the jury. My hands were sweating so much I used a whole box of Kleenex to dry them. On February 16, 1983, the jury, after three hours of deliberation, came in with guilty verdicts for both of us. When I heard the word, "guilty," my heart dropped. I broke down. It didn't make sense. This couldn't be happening to me. But it was happening to me.

It was the reality and no amount of crying could change that. I had no choice; I had to face the facts, ugly facts.

Specifically, I was found guilty of four charges: the murder and armed robbery of Lloyd Wickliffe and the attempted murder and armed robbery of Alvin Thompson.

Before court officers took me away, they let my mother, who was crying, hug me. I again told her what she already knew, that I was innocent. Having someone accused of murder in our family was all new to my mother. There were no murderers in our family. It was just unthinkable.

Next came the sentencing three weeks later on February 23, 1983. While one jury decided on our guilt or innocence, two separate juries[21]—one for Hope and one for me—would consider whether to invoke the death penalty.

I was, obviously, extremely nervous. I said to myself, "They are trying to kill me." My hands were sweating again. One of the juries recommended the death penalty for Hope. He had already been sentenced to death four months earlier for the fatal shooting of Officer Doyle on the CTA bus. He was scheduled to be executed by electric chair April 15.

We called a number of witnesses to testify on my behalf before the other jury would decide my fate. My mother was asked how she would feel if I were sentenced to death. She said:

"I really don't know. It has taken a lot out of me. But, I would feel I have failed because nobody believed me when I told them my child was in the house. I just don't know how I would feel. I just don't know. I swear, I just don't know." Her words broke my heart.

In my case, the second jury deliberated for more than three hours on whether to have me killed. Finally, it reached a decision with the foreman addressing the judge with the following statement:

"We are unable to conclude unanimously that there is no mitigating factor or factors sufficient to preclude the imposition of a death sentence upon the defendant, Alton Logan.

---

21. In multiple defendant trials with the death penalty as an option, separate juries were required.

We cannot unanimously find that the court shall sentence the defendant to death."

My life was saved. I wouldn't be going to death row. I learned it was a very close call.

The jury had voted 10–2 for the death penalty. That spared me because the jury had to be unanimous on the death penalty. Two votes kept me from being executed by the state.

However, I didn't understand how one jury decided on the death penalty for Hope and the other saved me from death row by two votes when I was the one found guilty of firing the shotgun that killed Wickliffe.

The judge, before sentencing me, asked if I wanted to say anything. I did. I said, "I feel that no matter what I say, you're going to do what you feel within your heart is right. You have already made up your mind what you are going to do. So, I feel whatever I say is unnecessary.

"I am going to say this: I did not commit this murder. I did not kill that man. Understand what I'm saying. That's it."

Judge Bailey replied, "Okay," and sentenced me to natural life, plus twenty-five years for attempted murder and twenty-five years each for two counts of armed robbery.

I went back to my cell thinking, "As much as you want, you can't kill me." I said that to the guards and cops over and over again. I didn't stop.

I was relieved to escape the death penalty, but I had to deal with the reality that I would spend the rest of my life in prison. Yes, that was bad, yet as strange as it may seem, I also thought that a life sentence gave me a chance to prove my innocence. That was something I never stopped hoping for. I continued to believe throughout the years that I would be set free even though I came within two votes of being sent to death row.

I learned years later that Coventry was in court the day the jury deliberated whether to recommend the death penalty. He said he didn't want to be in court during the trial because that might have raised questions about why he was there. He came for the sentencing because he was worried the jury might vote that I should die.

He was quoted in an April 2008 story by the Associated Press as stating, "It's pretty creepy watching people deciding if they're going to kill an innocent man."

Coventry told Berl that the ethics code permits lawyers to breach confidentiality to prevent a death. If I had been sentenced to die, Coventry said, he would have tried to invoke that exception. He didn't believe a court would accept his reasoning because the provision to break confidentiality to prevent death meant that the death might be caused intentionally during the commission of a crime. It was not intended to be used for someone convicted of a capital crime. Coventry said he planned to raise the argument nevertheless.

Since the code of ethics permits lawyers to break their silence "to prevent reasonably certain death or substantial bodily harm," Coventry said:

"I concluded in my mind that [a death sentence] would cover Alton Logan if he had faced the death penalty. I [was] not sure the system would accept that but I was prepared to make it." He added that if I had been sentenced to death, he and Kunz would have sought a meeting with the Illinois governor to ask that my life be spared.

Berl also interviewed Kunz and his position on the issue was overall the same as Coventry's. Kunz said he probably would have come forward if I had been sentenced to death, adding, the case "made me crazy" over the years.

I was sent to the Joliet Correctional Center in Joliet, Illinois for two weeks before being transferred to the Pontiac Correctional Center in Pontiac, Illinois. I would spend the next twenty-five years in Pontiac and the Stateville Correctional Center in Crest Hill, Illinois.

5.

Appeal

I was a convicted murderer, found guilty of fatally shooting a security guard who was a moonlighting Cook County sheriff's deputy. If that wasn't enough, I was also found guilty of trying to kill his partner, plus I was convicted of two counts of armed robbery, charges related to the theft of the revolvers stolen from the two guards.

It was almost too much to process. I had to deal with that while sitting in a prison with thousands of others. There was little empathy to be had in prison. No one gave a damn if I was innocent or not. I didn't have a shoulder I could cry on. The point is that I didn't get much support, reassurance or calls to "hang in there" from my cellmates. Since I had been in prison before, I knew I had to stand on my own two feet. If I showed any weakness, I wouldn't survive.

My hopes were transferred from a jury to the appeals process. The process, I was advised, was legally very complicated, and worse, would take lots of time. You sit and wait for months, even years, for decisions. Your hopes were raised when you expected a decision, and quickly dashed when appeals were denied. It was a real letdown to hear the court rejected your appeal, and sometimes I couldn't even understand the reasons. I suffered from a roller coaster of emotions.

The first step for me was to file papers that I was indigent and couldn't afford an attorney. My mother had spent $10,000 for legal expenses. Also, relatives and friends contributed to my legal fund. I was broke.

As a result, a Cook County public defender was appointed to represent me. An appeal was filed with the Illinois Appellate Court that three years later—let me emphasize that—three years later, on January 14, 1986, denied my appeal.

The court said, to summarize, that the identifications of me as the shooter in McDonald's by three witnesses at trial were reliable, and that the "overwhelming" testimony along with the evidence (What evidence? There was none.) established my guilt "beyond a reasonable doubt." One month later, we filed what is known as a petition for leave to appeal to the Illinois Supreme Court. The court denied our request on April 2, 1986.

I had already been in prison for four years. My lawyer tried to keep my hopes alive by telling me additional appeals could and would be made. I prayed that future efforts wouldn't be as futile as this one. It was very difficult to keep an optimistic outlook.

As I tried to deal with the rejections, something happened in Hope's case that opened an important door for me. His verdict and sentence were automatically appealed because he was on death row. The lawyers explained this was standard procedure.

The Illinois Supreme Court overturned his conviction because of errors in the trial court. Specifically, the court said the judge erred in admitting testimony from the victims' families during the guilt-innocence stage of Hope's trial, and the court ruled that this error was committed intentionally.

That argument—the use of testimony from victims' families—had not been raised in my appeal. My lawyer screwed up. To her credit, my assistant public defender filed an affidavit in which she acknowledged her mistake in not raising this issue for me.

As a result, the Supreme Court sent my case to the State Appellate Defender[22] and asked it to file a post-conviction petition. This petition would allow my attorneys to seek new evidence they might present, along with a demand for a new trial, to the court that convicted me.

My case went to Barbara Kamm, who worked diligently and passionately. She left no stone unturned. Right from the start, she told me she had heard "on the street" that some kind of legal document existed regarding my case, an affidavit that was locked in a strongbox.

---

22. Usually, the Cook County Public Defender's office would handle my case since it was responsible for post-conviction petitions in Cook County. In this case, the Supreme Court appointed the State Appellate Defender, which dealt with appeals statewide. The court offered no explanation.

Kamm said, "There were some affidavits in a box that can't be revealed at this time." She picked up that kind of stuff from several attorneys, some of whom said I was innocent. Of course, these rumors made us more than curious. It would be years before we found out what they meant.

On July 26, 1988, another two years later, Kamm filed a post-conviction petition in the Cook County Circuit Court. She made three major points:

The appellate attorney was ineffective for failing to raise the issue on which Hope was granted a new trial; the court should have allowed evidence connecting Andrew Wilson to the murder weapon; and the sentencing court considered matters outside of the record.

At an evidentiary hearing, we called as a witness the assistant public defender who messed up. She testified to her mistake.

A year later, on May 18, 1989, the court rejected Kamm's argument about my lawyer's ineffectiveness, stating that attorneys didn't have to raise every issue; they had to make choices. In denying us a new trial, the court also said the evidence was overwhelming as to my guilt.

Kamm continued the fight by appealing to the Appellate Court on the denial of my post-conviction petition. We got some good news two and a half years later. This court, on December 31, 1991, reversed the Circuit Court decision. It ruled that if the issue of victims' family testimony had been raised, there was a "reasonable probability" that my case would have been reversed. The court noted that "Logan challenged the sufficiency of the evidence against him in his original appeal and present appeal."

The Appellate Court gave me the best decision: it ordered a new trial for me and that the ballistics test on the shotgun and the cartridge shell should be admitted as evidence.

6.

Second Trial, 1994

I was excited about my second trial, which began with jury selection on August 12, 1994, about twelve years after my arrest. Maybe things would be different this time. I still retained some hope. I wasn't as nervous as in the first trial, but I still distrusted the system. I had learned too much. Unfortunately, it became clear to me pretty fast as I heard the testimony that it would be a replay of the first trial.

The only difference was that Charles Trent, one of three witnesses who identified me as the shooter, had died and one of my alibi witnesses, my mother's friend, Rosetta Johnson, had passed away. Also, I had new attorneys, James A. Sorensen and Steven M. Wagner,[23] both appointed by the court. The court assigned Sorensen and Wagner because the Public Defender's Office was representing Edgar Hope, and it would have been

---

23. Steven M. Wagner, a Cook County Circuit Court associate judge in Rolling Meadows, Illinois when we worked on this book in 2015, said since he was a judge, he had a policy not to talk about cases he'd handled as a lawyer.

a conflict of interest, since the cases overlapped, to represent me simultaneously.

Other than that, it was all too familiar. Alvin Thompson still maintained that I had fired the fatal shot at his partner. So did Anthonette Dawson. Only in this trial, she even added facts—more lies—to her story. This time she testified that I was in McDonald's with Hope and that she had seen me with him in the neighborhood. As I said, I had never met this man before I was put in the cell with him.

During cross-examination, she said she had testified to my relationship with Hope at the first trial as well. Again, that wasn't true. There was talk of charging her with perjury, but perjury charges were never filed.

The judge, Vincent M. Gaughan, unlike Judge Bailey in the first trial, did permit the shell and shotgun to be admitted as evidence. This was proof that it was Andrew Wilson who killed Wickliffe. Judge Gaughan refused to admit evidence on the relationship between Hope and Wilson, and he also barred testimony that there was a physical resemblance between Wilson and me. Both these points were important in proving my innocence.

Introducing the Hope–Wilson relationship was crucial because they had committed many other crimes together, and the fact that I looked somewhat like Wilson was important because the jury would understand how the eyewitnesses could have been mistaken.

In an interview with Berl in April 2017, Sorensen, then supervising attorney in the Maryland Public Defender's Office, said that while Judge Gaughan permitted the shotgun and shell to be introduced as evidence, he barred the defense from pursuing the fact that Wilson was in possession of the shotgun and other weapons found in the beauty shop owned by Wilson's aunt.

Sorensen told Berl, "We wanted to use the guns to show a connection between Wilson and Hope and that this was a gang connection, but we were cut off at the knees by the judge." Sorensen said the judge would not let him and Wagner follow up with that argument.

"We wanted to show that if the shotgun belonged to our guy, he would be in possession of it, not Wilson. But we were unable to do that." The judge's refusal to permit the defense to introduce the physical resemblance between me and Wilson and the Hope–Wilson longstanding criminal partnership, created additional "problems," Sorensen said.

Sorensen said uncorroborated eyewitness testimony "is always suspect although in this case it was very powerful. I knew it would be an uphill battle," he said.

Sorensen said he learned about the Kunz–Coventry affidavit from the *60 Minutes* program. He said he knew the two attorneys (Kunz and Coventry).

Arguing strongly on behalf of client-attorney confidentiality, Sorensen commended Coventry and Kunz. He said their actions were "brilliant" because without violating their ethical responsibilities they saved proof in such a way that their client knew exactly what was going to happen, but not until a time when it couldn't affect him.

"If there is no client-attorney confidentiality about everything, the relationship breaks down. It's confidentiality that they were protecting. I thought that was skillful, innovative, and intelligent. I give them all the credit in the world."

Then Sorensen added, "I am very happy that in the end the right thing happened."

With testimony and arguments completed, the case went to the jury. I worked hard to remain upbeat. It wasn't easy though. My hands were not sweating as they had before. Sure enough, the jury found me guilty on August 17, 1994, on the same four charges as in the first trial: murder and armed robbery of Lloyd Wickliffe, and attempted murder and armed robbery of Alvin Thompson. Despite my efforts to show no emotion, I broke down again. I couldn't help it even though the verdict wasn't a total surprise. I had seen all this before.

Sentencing was scheduled for November 1, 1994. The only good news was that since the jury in my first trial couldn't decide that there were "aggravating and mitigating factors" that justified putting me to death, the death penalty wasn't an option—it wasn't on the table—this time. My attorney, Jim Sorensen, made a plea for the judge to give me a sentence that would provide me a chance of being released before I died. He asked the judge to consider a sentence of forty years, stating such a sentence would make me eligible for parole at age seventy. Sorensen said: "To think he would be a threat to society or danger at age seventy is ridiculous.

"All we are asking you to do is set a sentence in this matter," Sorensen said, "that would give him an out date, give him and his family a glimmer of hope, give him something to work towards."

Before sentencing, the judge permitted me to speak, and I made the following statement:

> Ms. [Virginia] Bigane, Mr. [Earl] Grinbarg,[24] Mr. Sorensen, your honor. I first would like to thank Mr. Sorensen for representing me in this matter. Even though we weren't able to achieve the objectives I wanted, he did a remarkable job. Ms. Bigane, Mr. Grinbarg, I would like to commend them on their job. They did a good job.
>
> Anything I might have done during the course of this trial, I apologize for. Your honor, as I stated in the first trial and will state again, I had no knowledge of this crime or no participation. I understand the pain that Ms. Wickliffe is going through because my mother went through the same thing even though no one was ever found for the murder of my father. I know what she is feeling. That's all I would like to say.[25]

---

24. Assistant state's attorneys.

25. As we worked on the book, I couldn't remember what I did during the trial that had me apologize for my actions, nor why I commended the very prosecutors who succeeded in having me convicted—even though I was innocent. I have no idea why I did that. As to Steve Wagner, in the moment, I forgot to thank him.

My statement and the plea from my attorney fell on deaf ears. As I indicated, the death sentence was, thank God, not an option and the judge responded accordingly:

> Mr. Logan, I am moved by your statement, but nobody takes any pleasure in this, especially not me, to sentence another human being. I sentence you to natural life for the murder of Lloyd Wickliffe, and 25 years in the state penitentiary on the charge of armed robbery of Lloyd Wickliffe; 25 years for the attempted murder of Alvin Thompson and 25 years for the armed robbery of Alvin Thompson. These are to run concurrently with the counts of murder.

Judge Gaughan gave me basically the same sentence I received at the first trial. He decided, as did Judge Bailey, that I should die in prison.

My relatives, who were by my side in court every day, were heartbroken. Their hopes were dashed again. Once more, my family had to accept injustice from our justice system, and it was a pill they had a hard time swallowing. My mother heard she would never see her son except behind prison walls.

I went back to my cell feeling depressed, angry, and bitter. I had to come to grips with the fact that I would never walk out of prison a free man. Accepting that reality wasn't an easy thing to do.

7.

Prison Life

I was shocked when I was found guilty in the first trial, and even more devastated—if that was possible—after the second conviction. All I could think of is that I would live in a cell for who knew how many years. I didn't understand it no matter how hard I tried. I knew I had to prepare myself mentally for a life in prison. Why? Because if you aren't mentally ready, it'll destroy you.

The fact that I had served five years in prison from 1975–80 was good and bad. It was good because unlike those who were never incarcerated, I knew what to expect. I could "prepare" myself somewhat. It was bad because I understood all too well what I would have to endure, possibly, until I died. That thought didn't sit well with me. I would live in one of the most miserable and dangerous environments anywhere.

I could write a book on prison life alone. Those who say that my life sentence was better than the death penalty are out of their minds. The only difference between the two is that if you're sentenced to death, it is quicker. A life sentence is just as bad as a death sentence. With a life sentence, it just takes longer for you to die.

The conditions, to understate it, are not conducive to rehabilitation. You are constantly on lockdown and ordered where to go, at what time to go, when to stand up, or sit down. A cell for two people was eight by ten feet; some were only five by eight. It is hot in the summer; cold in winter. It was infested with roaches and mice. We had a sink and metal toilet. I could hang a sheet in front of the toilet for privacy.

Not only are you incarcerated—behind steel bars—but, as I said, you're living in a very dangerous place. You spend a lot of time working to survive. Like other prisoners, I carried a shank I made from scrap metal that I snuck into my cell. I always kept it with me, and it was under my pillow when I slept.

For 24/7, you just work to stay alive. That is all you think about. All your energy is devoted to making sure you don't make a mistake—a fatal one. The minute you leave your cell, you're in danger. You can get caught up in situations you know nothing about and it can cost you your life.

I stayed out of trouble by learning how to observe. You keep an eye on everything that's around you. After all, you're in prison with hardened criminals: murderers, rapists, arsonists, child molesters. By keeping alert, I could tell when "something" was about to happen, and I stayed clear of the upcoming trouble. Prison, after all, is a place where drugs are prevalent, fights break out constantly. Guards are beaten to an inch of their lives, and I saw prisoners killed. With all due respect to authorities, if the objective is to rehabilitate people, then prison is hardly the right place in which to do it.

I also worked to build good relationships with other prisoners. I made a lot of friends, which helped me cope.

It is true that I was still thankful to receive a life sentence. The reason was that I always believed someone, sooner or later, would come forward and say something that would free me. I always believed that. My faith never wavered that the facts would come out. My mother told me repeatedly that one day truth would prevail. I was convinced of that; I shared her faith.

After my first conviction, I was sent to the Joliet Correctional Center in Joliet, Illinois. It was a prison for receiving prisoners and at which they decided how long you would stay and where to send you. Much depended on whether you were a new prisoner or one who had done time before. I was at Joliet for a few weeks before I was sent to the Pontiac Correctional Center in Pontiac, Illinois. I was in Pontiac from 1983 to 1997 before I was transferred to the Stateville Correctional Center, where I stayed until my exoneration in 2008.

From the first day that I stepped into my cell at Pontiac, I felt only anger and frustration. My anger took control of me. I couldn't understand why I was in jail, why I would be in jail for the rest of my life. I was twenty-eight years old, and a life sentence meant I could be in prison for fifty years or more, depending on how long I would live.

I was innocent. I didn't commit the murder. I was never in the McDonald's. I had never even met Edgar Hope or Andrew Wilson. The cops and prosecutors had no proof. There was no question they knew I didn't do the crime.

In my anger, I gave everyone a hard time. I talked back constantly to the guards and broke rules. I did a lot of stupid stuff. I insisted they weren't going to tell me what to do. I would decide what to do. If the guards ordered me to do "X," I would do "Y." If they said, "sit down," I would stand up. I was determined to fight the system, not realizing I was only hurting myself. The guards couldn't have cared less about my attitude. They had the power to get even, lots of power.

As a result, during the first five years, I spent a lot of time in segregation—referred to as "seg" by prisoners. The public calls it solitary confinement. I would spend as much as thirty days at a time in seg. I was alone in a cell. I passed the time smoking, reading, and pacing the cell. I also had a TV. I was let out for five hours one day a week to walk in the yard. I was also permitted to take a shower once a week. If I added up all the time I spent in seg, I think it would total about three and a half years.

I could talk to prisoners across from me and those on either side of me. We even played chess, calling out the moves we wanted to make. It wasn't total isolation.

My mother and other relatives visited me monthly. It was about a two-hour drive to the prison from Chicago. It really upset my mother when she saw me wearing an orange jumpsuit.

Prisoners had to change into the jumpsuit from the denim blue prison uniforms when they were taken to solitary. She didn't like thinking of me alone in a cell and pleaded that I try to get along with the guards. She finally warned me that she wouldn't visit me anymore if she saw me wearing the orange jumpsuit.

I fought the system for about five years. I sure wasn't going to complain. I wanted to show that I was tough and could take it. The message I wanted to send was that, "You can't break me." I must admit, it was hard on me. It ain't easy sitting behind bars alone, especially when you know you're innocent. You rethink and rethink the events, and no matter how many times you do that, you still can't understand how you ended up in prison.

It took a while but I finally realized that I wasn't going to win this fight; I would be the only one to pay a price. If I didn't change my attitude, not only would I continue to do time in seg, but I worried that if my case went back to court, the authorities would review my prison record, and if officials read that I continually spent time in segregation, it wouldn't help me get any sympathy or favorable judgments.

I adjusted to my reality, and worked to keep myself busy. I shared my story with cellmates. The other prisoners, however, showed little interest because some of them claimed to be innocent as well. Since I had firsthand experience with being convicted while innocent, I considered that the stories I heard might have been true. I didn't reject them out of hand. My situation may not have been unique. As to sympathy, well, I wasn't going to get that in prison.

One major step I took was to join the Gangster Disciples (GD), a gang that was founded in the 1960s on Chicago's south side. It had a presence in many U.S. cities, and, I believe, all the prisons in Illinois. I joined the GD primarily for protection.

With about 500 members in our prison, the GD was highly organized, requiring the payment of dues and strict adherence to its bylaws. There were other gangs in prison, and in this tense environment, I wanted to make sure someone had my back. The GD did.

I worked to take control of my anger and turn my prison life around. I went to school and got a GED, which is the equivalent to a high school diploma. I earned an associate of applied science certificate and a certificate for building maintenance under programs sponsored by MacMurray College, of Jacksonville, Illinois. I finished a course in heating and air-conditioning put on by the Lincoln Technical Institute, which had a campus in Melrose, Illinois. I took courses in carpentry, electrical installation, typing, and welding. I also spent time in the woodworking shop. I even made some crosses and replicas of the Bible, which I sent to family members.

I was doing well, so well that one evaluation on a resume prepared by the prison stated that "[he] gets along well with others, able to do and adjust to any job, willing to help others and knows about shop safety."

I was trying my best to make the most of my prison life.

A typical day consisted of the following: I was out of my cell by 8:30 a.m. and in school until 3:30 p.m. After classes, I went to the yard. I also spent lots of time in the law library where I did research, hoping I might find something that would help my case.

Unfortunately, when I found issues that weren't raised in the first appeal and told the attorney who had worked on my appeal, she got mad. I learned she was only one year out of law school. After that, I was lucky that Barbara Kamm, the assistant appellate defender, was assigned to my case. She was excellent and I continually gave her ideas resulting from my research.

I went to church in prison, but sometimes I became very frustrated and I couldn't enjoy the service. Most attended church to mingle with other prisoners, not to pray. It wasn't a pleasant religious experience.

I started studying Islam. I reflected back on what I had been told about the religion, that it was a radical religion. It wasn't. I discovered that Islam and Christianity were the same; both teach the same thing. Both teach love. I thought briefly about converting, but I didn't. I remained a Baptist.

My religion helped me get me through my ordeal. Yes, it did; yes, it did. It didn't matter whether I was Baptist or Muslim. I read the Bible continually in my cell. Because of my faith, I knew that all the individuals who worked to get me home came into my life for that purpose. God put them in that place, in my life.

Most important were the visits from my mother, Aunt Barbara, and my brother, Tony. Whenever they came, I made sure to look happy. I put on a good front because I didn't want to worry them. I guess it worked because my aunt told Berl in interviews he conducted with her that when she saw me, I was always happy. She added that I was "probably keeping it all inside." Also, mail was very important to me. Letters were my contact with the outside world. I spent a lot of time writing to relatives and friends.

Periodically, of course, my anger would return. At times—not often—I couldn't control my emotions. For instance, I was angry when prison officials refused to let me go to the funeral of my grandmother, Pauline Gordon, when she died in 1985 because, I was advised, that the woman who helped raise me—my grandmother!—wasn't part of my "immediate family."

In late 1995, my aunt, Barbara Cannon, gave me very sad news in a telephone call: my mother was dying of breast cancer. With my mother on her deathbed, the authorities offered me the choice: visit her—for all of fifteen minutes—before she died, or attend her funeral. I was furious. My aunt urged me to see her one last time, and she was right, of course. I chose to visit my mother.

I was shackled like a dog when prison guards transported me to Michael Reese Hospital on the south side of Chicago. My hands were cuffed and the handcuffs were attached to a chain that went around my waist. My legs were also bound together with a chain. That is how I saw my dying mother.

We couldn't even hold hands because of the chains, shackles, and handcuffs. She urged me to keep my hopes up, and, after fifteen minutes, I was returned to the prison. I saw my mother in the first week of January 1996. She died two weeks later on January 22.

I had a major health scare in Stateville in 2007 about a year before I was freed. I was in my cell when I had chest pains. I had an examination at the prison hospital. A nurse said I was suffering from "gas," and I was returned to my cell.

I complained again about the pains in the morning. Doctors performed an EKG, and I was immediately transferred to another hospital where I received a stent implant. After I woke up in recovery, one of the police officers who took me to the hospital called me the "lion hearted" because, he said, the entire right side of my heart had stopped working. I was hospitalized for about two weeks. (Another stent along with a defibrillator were implanted about a year after my release.)

I have often thought that if my problem hadn't been diagnosed properly after I complained of pains a second time, I might have died in prison and my innocence would never have been proven.

8.

More Appeals and Post-Conviction Efforts

After the second conviction, I would be at the mercy of the time-consuming, very frustrating appeal process again. My case went back to Barbara Kamm in the State Appellate Defender's office.

Kamm immediately initiated two steps: Because I was broke, she "ghost-wrote" a post-conviction petition for me, which I filed *pro se*[26] on October 21, 1997, and, at the same time, she submitted a new appeal.

In the appeal, she argued that I was denied a fair trial because: I wasn't permitted to present "relevant evidence to show that Andrew Wilson committed this offense [the murder at McDonald's] with Edgar Hope, and Logan [I] was misidentified." She cited numerous examples.

Kamm's appeal was rejected on December 22, 1997, three

---

26. A filing in which I stated that I didn't have any funds, and in which I was requesting legal counsel.

years after my second conviction. The court held that there was no error in precluding evidence pertaining to Andrew Wilson because I was allowed "to present substantial amount of evidence in support of the defense of mistaken identity." Numerous other of our arguments were also rejected.

As a result of my *pro se* petition, the Cook County Public Defender's office was appointed to assist me on a post-conviction petition. My case was supervised by Harold J. Winston who, along with his staff, worked tirelessly on my behalf. Kamm volunteered to continue to help. Erica L. Reddick, assistant public defender,[27] was originally assigned to my case and Winston, after he became the unit supervisor in early 2000, agreed to serve as cocounsel and lead attorney. Joining the defense team were Noel Zupancic, an investigator, Christine Komperda, a paralegal, and Elizabeth Turillo, a senior law student who conducted research and drafted documents.

For the next eight years, from 2000–2007, Winston's group: reinterviewed witnesses, sought out possible new ones, interviewed prisoners, and reviewed transcripts and police reports. Winston's team achieved good results, getting affidavits from the following people:

- Gail Hilliard, who was a McDonald's employee and was working the night of the shooting. She swore that I wasn't in the restaurant at the time of the

---

27. She became a Cook County Circuit Court judge.

murder, stating, when shown a photo of me, "There's no doubt in my mind that Andrew Wilson was the person who pulled out the sawed-off shotgun and shot Lloyd Wickliffe on Jan. 11, 1982." She had not been interviewed before by any of my attorneys.

- Thomas Bennett, who was a Chicago detective on my case in 1982. He said when he visited a dying friend, Charles R. Grunhard, also a detective, in Mountain Home, Arkansas, Grunhard told him that while he and Burge were drinking, Burge admitted that police had the wrong man in the McDonald's case and the right man was Andrew Wilson. (Grunhard died in 1990.) Bennett also said when he first interviewed Anthonette Dawson, one of the three witnesses who identified me as the killer, she didn't tell him she knew who fired the shotgun at Wickliffe. However, in later interviews, she accused me of killing Wickliffe.

- Terrance "Terry" Babers, Dawson's boyfriend, who contradicted Dawson's testimony. He said Dawson didn't mention she knew who the shooter was, or that she ever saw me and Hope together.

- Pamela Johnson,[28] who was working as a cashier in McDonald's the night of the shooting, but wasn't called as a witness at either of my trials. She said she "did not see Alton Logan" in the restaurant that night.

---

28. When she worked at McDonald's, she was Pamela Parker.

Winston and Zupancic went to three different prisons to interview inmates. Two signed affidavits that Hope and/or Wilson had told them I was innocent and the third said he was aware of an affidavit that Wilson had drafted in which he confessed to the crime, and exonerated me. (I discuss that affidavit in Chapter 11.)

The defense team found huge gaps in police files. Many reports were missing and even former Police Superintendent Richard J. Brzeczek testified at one hearing that the reports should have been in the files.

I have outlined in some detail the appeals and post-conviction processes to show how time-consuming they are, and why my emotions fluctuated wildly with spirits rising when appeals were filed, and crushed when courts rejected our arguments.

I rested my hopes on Winston and his staff finding evidence that might get me another—yes, a third—trial. My lawyers were vigilant in their attempts to do so.

We also lost time on some procedural matters. For instance, we filed a motion in 2002 to have a special prosecutor take over the case because the head of the Cook County State's Attorney Office, Richard Devine, had once represented Jon Burge. In April, Cook County Circuit Court Judge Paul Biebel, Jr., assigned the case to the Attorney General's Office, which handled the prosecution for the next six years (2002–08.) I think this was the right thing to do, but the move didn't mean much as to my legal efforts to get a third trial, and it slowed the process.

As we searched for legal avenues we might pursue, I had an idea. I had read about DNA testing and how it was being used to prove innocence or guilt. The DNA science began to be applied in criminal investigations in the 1970s and became more sophisticated in the '80s. I asked my attorneys to see if we could conduct some DNA testing on the shotgun and the shell found in McDonald's. Maybe, just maybe, we could find Wilson's DNA on both, or even just the shell or the shotgun. The attorneys agreed with me and started the process. Sure, the odds were not good. But we had nothing to lose if we didn't find anything.

As we worked on new legal strategies, I got a most unbelievable break, one that no one could have predicted. It had nothing to do with evidence, witnesses, police reports, affidavits, or court proceedings, and it proved that my mother was right when she repeatedly told me, "The truth will come out one day."

9.

Affidavit Discovered

Harold Winston, the lead attorney on my defense team, was heading home on the Burlington Northern Santa Fe (BNSF) train at about 5:30 p.m. He sat down when a Page One story in *The Chicago Reader* caught his attention. Under the headline, "The Persistence of Andrew Wilson," the lead of the story by John Conroy on November 29, 2007, read:

> Andrew Wilson, the notorious killer of Chicago police officers William Fahey and Richard O'Brien, is dead. Wilson, who was serving a life sentence at Menard Correctional Center, died of natural causes November 19 in a hospital in Belleville, Illinois.

In other reports on Wilson's death, Derek Schnapp, a spokesman for the Illinois Department of Corrections, said Wilson had been dealing with "health related" issues. Schnapp refused to elaborate because Wilson's family didn't want the cause revealed.

The Reader story reminded Winston that someone over the years had suggested that if Wilson died in prison, he should contact Wilson's 1982 attorneys (Dale Coventry and Jamie Kunz) about my case. In our interviews with Winston, he couldn't remember who gave him this advice. He said it might have been people in his office or a paralegal who heard it from someone who had talked with Jamie Kunz.

Coventry was unequivocal in our interviews that he never talked with anyone about the affidavit and its contents, and Andrea Lyon also maintained she never broke her silence. Kunz, however, acknowledged that he mentioned it many times to friends and associates. If the subject of innocent people serving prison sentences was discussed, he would say he knew of such a situation. He would talk about my case but didn't mention any names.

"I talked about it . . . in the course of these years . . . at least to say I know of a case where a guy's serving a natural life sentence for a crime he didn't do and the reason I know is that my client did it, and told me he did it, and I can't talk about it," Kunz said. "I've been fairly discreet about that, moved mostly by self-pity, and besides, it's a cracking good story. Coventry swears up and down he didn't talk and I believe him. Put the blame on me. I'll take it."

His stories may have reached the person who advised Winston to contact Coventry and Kunz.

Kunz may also have been the source of rumors Barbara Kamm heard about some kind of "secret affidavit" testifying to my innocence.

Whoever was the source of the advice to contact Coventry and Kunz, Winston, when he reached his office the next day, called Coventry.[29] He wasn't in, so Winston left a message. Coincidentally, Kunz called Winston on another matter. The two decided to meet at Kunz's home to discuss Wilson's death and what it might mean for me.

Kunz briefed Winston about the affidavit and that Wilson confessed to Kunz and Coventry that, "I was the guy with the shotgun." Winston telephoned Coventry who said he wouldn't release the affidavit voluntarily. He asked Winston to file a motion for disclosure and have a judge order him to do so.

Coventry said, in his interviews with Berl, he wanted to make sure that everything would be done properly and legally, that there would be no mistakes. "I was taking every legal step I could to make sure it would work. I was trying to make it as legal as possible to avoid any challenges and to make sure it would be OK.

"The issue was whether I would volunteer information and the answer was, 'No.' But, do I respond to a court order and the answer is, 'Yes.'"

I found out that Wilson died at about the same time, and

---

29. If Winston had not called Coventry about Wilson's death, Coventry said his plan was to have someone notify Winston and ask him to call him (Coventry). Coventry didn't want to call himself, Coventry continued, because he didn't want to give the appearance that it was his case; it was Winston's.

I called Winston, who confirmed Wilson's death. He said he already knew about it, and that he had talked to Coventry and planned a meeting with him.

The next thing I remember was that Winston called to notify me about the affidavit. He summarized what Kunz had said about the document. I wasn't sure what it might mean. I didn't know much about the law. Yes, it sounded good. Yet, I didn't want to be too happy. I had been through too much.

Finally, I said to myself, someone has come forward and told the truth. I've been saying for more than twenty-five years, "It wasn't me." Winston also called members of my family to advise them about the affidavit, and he expressed hope that this would free me.

I felt a little optimistic. I knew it all depended on what the prosecutors would say—if this gets to court. They fought me all the way throughout the years. I was sure they would fight me again. I wasn't totally confident that the affidavit would help me.

I was also upset. If it was true that these lawyers had evidence that I was innocent, how could they not say anything for all those years? How could they keep quiet when they knew an innocent man was rotting in prison? I thought the following, "You know the facts, and still you don't come forward to let it be known." I couldn't understand that. Yes, later, when I learned why Coventry and Kunz kept silent, I gave them credit for following the rules. The attorneys were the only ones who did.

During the court hearings and the ensuing publicity, I read an Associated Press story that two years earlier—in about 2006—Kunz called Coventry to check on the affidavit. The two had not talked in about ten years.

In the story, Kunz is quoted as saying, "We're both getting along in years. You ought to do something with that affidavit to make sure it's not wasted in case we both leave this good Earth." Coventry assured Kunz that the affidavit was in a safe place. Coventry believed that if he died, and my case was still at issue, his daughter, also an attorney, would find it, decipher its meaning and take the appropriate actions. Kunz and Coventry didn't talk again until Winston called after Wilson's death.

On December 17, 2007, Winston filed a motion, asking the court to order disclosure of the affidavit. The motion summarized how I had maintained that I was innocent and recapped the entire case. It stated that Coventry and Kunz: ". . . have advised counsel (Winston) that they are willing to come forward and disclose what Andrew Wilson communicated to them [in March 1982] about his involvement in the McDonald's case if this court enters an order either directing or authorizing them to do so in the interests of justice."

The motion also pointed out why the order is permitted under the law and, most importantly, enumerated how at the second trial vital evidence was barred from being entered into the record. This evidence included the facts that:

- Wilson hid the shotgun he fired to kill Wickliffe in McDonald's in his aunt's beauty shop where it was found.
- Hope was a frequent partner of Wilson's in the crimes the two committed.
- Wilson planned to break Hope out of the Cook County Hospital, where he was recuperating from a gunshot wound suffered when he was arrested for killing a police officer on the CTA bus.
- One of the witnesses against me, Charles Trent, testified that Wilson and I had a similar appearance. That alone should have created doubt about his identification of me as the shooter.

The motion also cited other new evidence, including affidavits from several witnesses who stated that I wasn't in the McDonald's the night of the murder.

In making the case for disclosure, Winston wrote, "Freedom to make these disclosures may open up leads to additional evidence of Alton's innocence. An innocent man should not be left to languish in prison."

The case was assigned to Cook County Circuit Court Judge James M. Schreier and, from what I heard, I finally got a break—a big break.

Coventry told Berl that having Judge Schreier preside over the case, "was the best thing that could have happened to Alton Logan. Judge Schreier is one of the few completely honorable men in that court system."

On January 11, 2008—on the twenty-sixth anniversary of the murder—Judge Schreier granted our motion, stating, "Attorneys Dale Coventry and William Jameson Kunz are free to discuss what Andrew Wilson told them about his involvement in the shooting at McDonald's on January 11, 1982, with attorneys in this case." He ruled that Wilson had waived his attorney-client confidentiality privilege regarding the McDonald's murder once he died. Both Coventry and Kunz testified at that hearing about their conversation with Wilson.

My case was attracting public interest, and we were contacted by *60 Minutes*. The producer said they wanted to do a story on me. I think *60 Minutes* learned about my case from stories in Chicago media outlets. I told Winston I had no problem with doing that. The reporter, Bob Simon, first talked to Coventry and Kunz and later came to the Stateville Correctional Center in Crest Hill, Illinois to interview me.

The segment aired Sunday, March 9. As a result, that brought more attention to my unique situation, particularly in Chicago, and from then on I received lots of publicity. Most of it was very favorable, more than favorable. The public was outraged. No one could understand it. Kunz said years later, after my release, he didn't expect such a reaction. He said many demanded his and Coventry's disbarment, others recommended the two be fined, and some suggested that he and Coventry be imprisoned for twenty-six years.

"The feeling of release [when I was freed in 2008]," Kunz said, "was so powerful, I could live with the brickbats."

In his filing that the Kunz–Coventry affidavit should be admitted at our hearing, Winston also argued that extensive evidence existed that I didn't commit the murder. This evidence included:

- Sworn statements by a McDonald's employee, Gail Hilliard, that the man with the shotgun was Andrew Wilson. As I have mentioned, she hadn't been called previously to testify in my case. Her statement was corroborated by Pamela Johnson, also a McDonald's employee, who knew me. She said she didn't see me in the restaurant the night of the murder. I referred to her earlier as well.
- The fact that the shotgun used at McDonald's was found February 1982 along with guns belonging to the two police officers killed by Andrew Wilson in his aunt's beauty shop.
- Testimony by Donald White to whose home Wilson and Hope went after the shooting that Andrew Wilson committed the crime with Hope. We also had statements from his brothers as to my innocence.
- Wilson's involvement in several other crimes with Edgar Hope.

"Denying the admission of this affidavit and testimony would deprive Alton of his constitutional right to present a complete defense," Winston wrote. Winston stated that my rights had been "trampled on" at my trials when crucial evidence was barred from admission, witnesses on my behalf were not permitted to testify, and we were denied the right to challenge prosecution witnesses.

We presented an affidavit from Marc Miller dated February 25, 2008, in which he swore that Hope firmly maintained, in his second or third interview, that I was innocent. Hope didn't understand how I was charged, Miller stated in the affidavit. Hope didn't know who I was, and he gave him (Miller) names of people who would verify that he committed crimes only with Andrew Wilson.

Miller added that Hope "leaned" heavily on him to make sure he told Rimland that I was innocent, and that Rimland should do his job by conducting a thorough investigation to have the charges against me dropped. Miller acknowledged that he couldn't permit Hope to talk to Rimland.

"Because my conscience was troubled about what to do, I waited before I informed Rimland that his client, Alton Logan, was innocent," Miller swore in his affidavit.[30] He also said he let Jim Sorensen,[31] one of two lawyers in my second trial, know that I was innocent.

On March 10, Miller testified before Judge Schreier. Although he was living in Florida, he had called Winston and volunteered to come to court. At the hearing, Miller said that

---

30. As I noted in Chapter 3, Rimland said he was never contacted by Miller regarding my innocence.

31. Sorensen also told us he did not remember receiving such a call from Miller.

Hope denied ever having seen me before I was indicted for the McDonald's murder, and ordered him to tell Rimland that I was innocent. Hope also urged that Miller could go out into his neighborhood and verify what he was telling him about Wilson being his only partner.

Hope demanded, at least five or six times, that Miller see Rimland. "He was ordering, haranguing me to seek out Mr. Rimland," Miller testified.

Miller assured Hope he would do as he directed, i.e. tell Rimland about my innocence and check Hope's story in the neighborhood. He testified he went to meet Coventry and Kunz to tell them that, in fact, their client, Wilson, was guilty of the McDonald's murder.

Miller admitted he was "surprised, shocked, upset, concerned, confused about what I should be doing."

Miller said he did go to Hope's neighborhood and verified his client's story with at least one individual nicknamed "Black Tony" who confirmed that Hope was Andrew Wilson's right-hand man. It was several months later, he said, before he contacted Rimland.

After he told Rimland what Hope had said, Rimland asked to speak with Hope. Miller responded, "You know I can't let you do that." Miller acknowledged signing the affidavit drafted by Lyon and signed by Coventry and Kunz. He said he did so because, "I believe it to be the truth." He added that the attorneys created the affidavit because they were concerned about "the possibility of an innocent man going to the electric chair."

The front page of *The Chicago Sun-Times*, March 11, 2008. (Photograph courtesy of *Sun-Times Media*)

I never had any knowledge of or understood why Hope instructed his lawyer to pass along his message that I was innocent to my attorney. Ultimately, I was grateful, even though it took twenty-six years to free me. I never found out why he did it. After we were tried together in 1983 and briefly shared a cell, I never saw him again. Hope died March 24, 2012, in the Menard Correctional Center in Chester, Illinois. He was fifty-two.

The day after my hearing, on March 11, to my pleasant surprise, *The Chicago Sun-Times*, which was published in a tabloid format, devoted the entire front page to my story. It ran my photo for half the page next to a huge headline that stated, "Let Him Go."

Inside, on Page 4A, the paper published a summary news story on my ordeal, and in an editorial in the same edition, *The Sun-Times* called for my release. The editorial stated:

> Let Alton Logan go. For 26 years—nearly half his life—this man has been trapped behind bars for a murder he insisted he did not commit. We believe Alton Logan was robbed of his freedom. Now Attorney General Lisa Madigan or Gov. [Rod] Blagojevich must release him.
>
> Though claims of innocence usually fall on deaf ears, Logan's claims ring achingly true.

The editorial expressed its sympathy for the lawyers who didn't speak up on my behalf because of lawyer-client confidentiality. The paper said it understood the moral dilemma the lawyers faced, adding, ". . . it galls us, offends us to the core, that an innocent man could rot in jail for 26 years though another man had confessed to the crime."

The editorial raised the question that Berl posed in his introduction regarding what the lawyers would have done if one of their loved ones had sat in prison under the same circumstances. Would they have remained silent?

"But imagine that Alton Logan were your brother or your father. Wouldn't you want to give Wilson's lawyers an ethical way out?" the paper asked in its concluding paragraph.

About ten days after this hearing, Winston unexpectedly received a letter from Philip W. McDowell, a prisoner and jailhouse lawyer in the Danville Correctional Center in Danville, Illinois. In the letter, McDowell wrote, "For Alton Logan's sake, please take seriously this letter and move Judge Schreier to immediately impound all [of] Mr. Wilson's personal effects whether released to family or still in IDOC [Illinois Department of Corrections] custody."

Why should Winston do this? Because, McDowell said,

Amongst his belongings (legal papers) a detailed sworn statement should be found in which Mr. Wilson clearly implicates himself and absolves your client of the 1982 Chicago McDonald's robbery during which Alvin Thompson and Lloyd Wickliffe were shot, Mr. Wickliffe fatally. How do I know of the affidavit? Because as his 'jailhouse lawyer' from 1998–2000, I wrote it.

In addition to Wilson's affidavit, McDowell said, is his own affidavit attesting to its authorship, that "I'd read aloud to Mr. Wilson [Wilson was illiterate] the contents of the affidavit and all the exculpatory statements he'd asked I memorialize in writing."

McDowell said if Wilson's affidavit was not found among Wilson's possessions, the document may have been sent to Betsy Cardona (he didn't explain the relationship to Wilson although Winston described her as one of Wilson's friends) or to attorneys John Stainthorpe and Allan Sincox, who, McDowell said, represented Wilson in different actions.[32]

McDowell said, "Since it is in Mr. Logan's interest that I write, I have sent a copy of this letter to Judge Schreier, Dale Coventry and Jamie Kunz so as to ensure you do not summarily dismiss the matter. Good luck and Godspeed in your search."[33]

On March 24, Winston filed a motion with Judge Schreier in which he asked the judge to order that Wilson's belongings be allowed to be inspected. Judge Schreier signed such an order, and Winston along with state attorneys, on April 27, searched through Wilson's possessions.

The lawyers didn't find the affidavit. Much later, we did get an unsigned copy of the affidavit from attorneys who would file a civil suit against the City of Chicago after my exoneration. I discuss Wilson's affidavit and why, according to McDowell, Wilson wrote it in Chapter 11.[34]

---

32. Berl contacted both attorneys in Chicago. The two told him they didn't have the affidavit, nor did they ever see it. Neither knew who Betsy Cardona was, and Berl couldn't find her.

33. In an exchange of letters with Berl, Philip McDowell said he learned of the Coventry/Kunz/Miller/Lyon affidavit from an article in *The Illinois Bar Journal*. McDowell said the article informed him for the first time that Wilson was dead. McDowell said, in one letter to Berl, that he wrote to Winston, "because I certainly would want someone to do so if they had information pertaining to my own case—of which I've long claimed to be innocent (but that's another story)."

34. Winston filed three affidavits signed by McDowell relating to Wilson's affidavit in Judge Schreier's court. In one of them, McDowell wrote that Wilson received a letter from Richard S. Kling, clinical law professor at the Chicago–Kent College of Law, asking him (Wilson) to "confess to several years earlier committing a homicide other than that of which Andrew, was convicted." In a deposition, which I discuss in Chapter 11, taken by the law firm that would file a civil rights suit on my behalf, McDowell stated more specifically that Kling asked Wilson to confess to the murder of Wickliffe and implicate me.

As these events unfolded, my Aunt Barbara sent me a letter in which she urged me "to be strong." She wrote: "It is not as long as it has been. You just hold on. Be encouraged. You are not alone. So many people are praying for you, good people. Don't be angry. Ask God to help you not be bitter or angry. I know it is hard."

She added, quoting Matthew 5:44, "God wants us to pray for those who disrespectfully use you." At that point, I wasn't prepared to pray for those who imprisoned me unjustly for more than two and a half decades.

I had to admit that things were looking up. All the hope I had maintained throughout the years seemed warranted. The truth was coming out. Winston made a copy of the Kunz–Coventry affidavit for me and while waiting for the next court hearing, I read it several times every day.

As I said in the preamble of this book, the entire document was just forty-five words. Those forty-five words cost me almost half of my life.

Despite all the good news, there was no way I could've predicted that at the next hearing, April 18, 2008, I would walk out of court a free man. True, I would be out on bail, but I was going home and not back to my cell.

10.

April 18, 2008 Hearing

On April 18, I worked the midnight shift at the Stateville Correctional Center in Crest Hill, Illinois, and in the morning, I boarded a prison bus for the ride to the Cook County Jail, which was near the courthouse. From there, I was taken to the courtroom. As I said at the end of the last chapter, I never dreamed that I would be set free. Never in a million years.

Because of all the publicity, the courtroom was packed. I couldn't believe the attention my case was getting. It felt good, very good. My family was there, and expected good news because Winston had called my relatives and said that I could be freed on bond. He even advised that they bring some civilian clothes and money to pay for a bond.

Even though I was skeptical about being released on bond, I wrote the following note to my brother, Eugene, who had flown in for the hearing from his home in Portland, Oregon: "If the judge gives me a bond can the family post it? From what my lawyer told me it would not exceed $2,000."

If the Judge gives me a bond can the family post it. From what my lawyer Told me. It would not exceed $2,000.

My brother, Eugene, saved this note in which I asked if the family could raise the money to get me out on bail, assuming the judge set a low bond.

Our job at this one-day hearing was to show that if the new evidence compiled by my attorneys had been available at my trials, there was a good chance the result would have been different—that I probably wouldn't have been convicted.

Appearing for the "people" were: Ellen Mandeltort, Richard D. Schwind, Vincenzo Chimera, and Jay Paul Hoffman. My defense team consisted of Winston, Erica L. Reddick, and Brendan P. Max.

Edgar Hope, who started this whole process in 1982 by instructing his attorney, Marc Miller, to tell my lawyer that I was innocent, was in court. On the advice of his counsel, Richard S. Kling, Hope refused to testify. He invoked his Fifth Amendment right against self-incrimination. He still had pending court proceedings relating to the murder of Police Officer Doyle on the CTA bus, which I mentioned early in this story.

Winston, in very eloquent introductory remarks, said, "No person convicted of a crime should be deprived of a life or liberty given compelling evidence of actual innocence."

Winston said that he would be presenting a variety of affidavits as exhibits proving my innocence. The affidavits were from:

- Ron Kliner, a prisoner, who said that Edgar Hope told him in July 2002 that I was innocent. Hope added, Kliner said, "I still can't believe he's in jail."

- Joseph Prendergast, a teacher, who said in his affidavit that he was tutoring Wilson to read when, one day, Wilson mentioned firing a shotgun at McDonald's. Prendergast never gave that statement much thought until late in 2007 when he read news articles about Wilson's death, and the article reported the McDonald's incident. He contacted Coventry and, ultimately, he came to the attention of the Public Defender's Office, and met with Winston, Reddick, and Zupancic.

- Philip McDowell who, in three affidavits, said that Wilson had him prepare an affidavit in which Wilson took responsibility for the McDonald's killing and stated that I was innocent. Wilson's signed and notarized affidavit was never found.

- Aryules Bivens, a prisoner, who attested to having a conversation in the late 1980s with Hope who told him I shouldn't be "in here . . . that's not his case. That's Gino's (Andrew Wilson's) case." He said Hope used the nickname "Head" when referring to me, and he, Bivens, didn't know who that was.

Years later, in late 1996, Bivens shared a cell with Wilson. During one conversation, he said, Wilson admitted he had "done a lot of cases and someone else is in the joint for one of them." Later, Wilson, Bivens said, identified me as being innocent of the murder he committed.

"I got pissed off and told him he has to do something about it!" Bivens wrote in his affidavit. "He laughingly said, 'Yeah. He'll get out over my dead body.'" Bivens said Wilson also bragged about a sawed-off shotgun and a police (long barrel) .38 being two of his "toys." Bivens said he was "coming forward because I don't believe an innocent man should be in prison." He added that he was continually being transferred between prisons, which kept him from speaking out earlier.

We would also call as a new witness—I mentioned her earlier—Gail Hilliard, a McDonald's employee who was in the restaurant when the shooting occurred and who had never testified before. On the witness stand, she was shown a photograph of Wilson, and she identified him as the shooter in McDonald's. She also said she had identified Wilson from a photograph in 1999 when Richard Kling, the lawyer representing Hope, interviewed her.

In his testimony, Prendergast stated that Coventry asked him to tutor Wilson in the fall in 1982 because Coventry thought that would help Wilson in his defense. He said he knew Coventry because they both had been teachers at a Chicago high school. He met with Wilson in the Cook County Jail twice a week in sessions lasting about 1½ hours each. He testified that at one tutoring session Wilson was very upset.

"He was very shaken," said Prendergast. "He looked like

a man who was about to burst into tears." When Prendergast asked Wilson why he was so distraught, Wilson said he had testified that day about torture he had suffered at the hands of police.

> He told me the police had attached alligator clips to his nose and that these were connected to a wire and crank box, and they cranked up the box. His head shook so much he didn't have a tooth in his head that wasn't loose.
>
> He showed me his teeth and how his teeth shook. He tore off his shirt and he showed me where the alligator clips had been attached to his nipples. He showed me burn marks where he said that he had been handcuffed to a radiator and left there. He got burned.
>
> Then he dropped his pants and he showed me where . . . he said . . . they attached alligator clips to his genitals. He showed me where the burn marks were.
>
> He was sobbing. He was just sobbing out loud. It was just big loud sobs. He began to pull his clothes back on, and he pulled up his pants and fastened them and got his shirt back on and he was sitting down.

Prendergast testified that he tried to console Wilson. When he did, Wilson responded—and this was an important statement: "Don't feel sorry for me. I am a really bad man. I fired a shotgun into a McDonald's restaurant, and there were children inside."

Prendergast said he never divulged to anyone what Wilson had told him about the McDonald's shooting. Like Winston, he learned of Wilson's death from the media, specifically in a story by Maurice Possley in *The Chicago Tribune.* Prendergast said he bought several papers and FedExed them to Coventry because he didn't know if Coventry was aware of the death, and he knew Coventry had a long history in Wilson's case.

"I was afraid he might not have received *The Tribune* out in the suburbs where he lived," Prendergast said.

After he read another story about Wilson that referred to the McDonald's incident, he informed Coventry about what Wilson had said. The article, also written by Possley, reported that I had been convicted of firing a shotgun into McDonald's and killing a guard.

"So, when I read that," Prendergast testified, "I realized that it was probably the same shotgun that Andrew Wilson fired and that the wrong man was in jail." With Coventry's help, Prendergast said he contacted the Public Defender's Office.

Prendergast did all this, he said, because he felt "an injustice had been done, and that I had information that could help right it."

I think Erica Reddick did an excellent job in presenting the testimony of Hilliard and Prendergast. I was feeling good, and I worked hard to keep my emotions in check. I didn't want to become overconfident. I understood that the system didn't give up very easily.

For instance, Assistant Attorney General Vincenzo Chimera argued that while Wilson told Prendergast he fired a shotgun into a McDonald's, "We don't know which McDonald's it was." Of course not. There were shotgun shootings at McDonald's all the time throughout the country. Also, Chimera certainly knew that the shotgun confiscated in the beauty shop where Wilson stayed was a match to the shell found at McDonald's. That match was confirmed six days after my arrest.

Chimera also said that Wilson told Prendergast there were children inside the restaurant. Chimera maintained Wilson was wrong: no children were in the McDonald's. These were the kind of nonsensical arguments I faced throughout all those awful years. It would've been funny if it hadn't been so sad and cost me half my life. What's more, all those who have had the misfortune of being caught up in the system have to put up with this kind of "justice."

Incidentally, if Chimera wanted to impugn the credibility of Wilson because he was wrong when he said children were inside the restaurant when there were none, he would also have had to question the veracity of Thompson, the guard who identified me as the killer. Why? Because just before being wounded and barely escaping a gunshot to the head, he pleaded with Hope not to "go back there and hurt any of the kids."

Sure enough, the prosecutors called as their one witness, Alvin Thompson, the security guard who was wounded and almost lost his life in McDonald's that night. He had identified me as the shooter when I was arrested as well as at my two trials. He was asked if he still believed it was me, and he answered, "Yes, I do."

On cross-examination, one of my assistant public defenders, Brendan P. Max, of the Forensic Science Division, pointed out Thompson had only seconds to see the shooter. Thompson himself admitted he saw the gunman for no "more than a second." Also, on the night of the incident, he described one of the two men to police officers, but he couldn't remember which of the two he was describing.

The prosecutors also submitted transcripts of previous testimony by witnesses who identified me as the killer.

In his summation, Winston pointed out that: there were discrepancies in eyewitness testimonies; that those who identified me only had a few seconds to do so; and, there was no physical evidence tying me to the crime. He also pointed to the credibility of Coventry, Kunz, and Marc Miller, and that Andrew Wilson had no reason to lie.

After my lawyers fought it out with the prosecutors, the judge complimented both sides for their professionalism. In announcing his decision, the judge said:

> Considering all the evidence in the case, all of the testimony, the record of the past two trials, it is the opinion of the Court that there is a reasonable probability that the guilty outcome of this case in the past would be different if the evidence produced at this post-conviction hearing were allowed to be introduced at any future trial.

Thus, concluding that there is a reasonable probability that the outcome would be something other than guilty, the Court orders first degree murder and other convictions in this indictment to be vacated, and a new trial ordered. The supplemental petition for post-conviction relief is granted.

The judge also observed that this had been a post-conviction hearing such as "I never experienced before." The judge set a $10,000 D bond. Sure, Winston told me the judge may set a low bond, but I didn't believe it. I said to myself, "Nah, no way. Not on a murder conviction. Never." I had no trust in the system. I had good reasons not to. Despite my pessimism, it did happen. I also knew that under a D bond I would only have to post ten percent to be released. I think the judge purposely set a D bond so that I might be able to raise the required $1,000.

Eugene, whom I had alerted to the possibility of a low bond, other members of my family, and friends went out into the hall and collected the money. Eugene told me that in addition to the money put into the pot from my relatives, contributions were made by people from the court gallery, sheriff's deputies, and department of corrections personnel.

There was so much confusion that I wasn't released right from the courtroom. Instead, the guards took me to a receiving area at the Cook County Jail where I waited for about three hours.

My aunt, Barbara Cannon, who was in the court gallery, wasn't angry with Coventry and Kunz. "They did what they had to do," she said in response to questions from reporters. My uncle from Milwaukee, Arthur Gordon, who provided $100 for the bail, had a different view. He said, "Justice had to be done. But to lay him there for twenty-six years, it makes me bitter.

"I knew he didn't do that because I had been talking to him over the years. He kept his spirit. He said, 'Uncle, I have to stay up. I can't go down. I can't go down.'"

In his interviews, my brother, Eugene, said: "Nobody deserves to be locked away for twenty-six years for something they didn't do. It's a blessing to me that my brother has been released. He's not been exonerated yet, but we're going back to court, and it will happen.

"I'm going to turn him on to life. That's what we're going to do. We're going to live it together."

My other brother, Tony, added, "Twenty-six years of his life . . . he didn't get a chance to raise a family, didn't get a chance to spend time with me and my younger brother [Eugene] here."

Other family members and friends in court that day were Terry Walker, whom I would marry in 2013, my uncle, Milan Cannon, and several cousins.

Interestingly, Jamie Kunz, one of Andrew Wilson's attorneys who signed the affidavit, was in the courtroom when bail was set. I read in the papers that he said, "The family was shedding tears, and so was I. I've known Logan was innocent for twenty-six years."

In the Cook County Jail, I changed into the clothes that my family had brought. The trouble was that the pants, belonging to my brother, Tony, were about three sizes too big, and I didn't have a belt. As we left the courtroom and talked to reporters, my aunt held up my pants from the back. I told her not to let go because I didn't want the papers to publish a photo of me with the pants around my shoes.

The judge asked with whom I would be staying. My aunt answered I would be living at her house. With the proceedings completed, I walked out with my relatives and friends.

Reporters were all over the place. Constantly, they asked me how it felt being released, and each time, I responded with a big sigh. "Fine, I am very happy," I repeated over and over again. There were lots of hugs, kisses, and tears.

I made a phone call and the media apparently listened in and reported that I called my "little sister." Of course, I didn't have a sister, only two brothers.

The quote in the papers said, "Sis, did you hear what I said? It's over with. I'm free. I no longer have to deal with it."

The statement is accurate, but the woman I called was Pricillia Roberts, a close family friend in San Antonio, Texas, whom I considered my godsister. She and Eugene had been classmates.

I was, of course, elated. I was free. It is very hard to describe my emotions. I shed many, many tears while popping candy into my mouth.

I got into a car—the first time I had been in one in twenty-six years—and we went to my aunt's house. Before we did, I

We are leaving the courtroom April 18, 2008, after I was released on a $1,000 bond. I have my arm around my aunt, Barbara Cannon, and my brother, Tony (right). My other brother, Eugene, who flew in from Portland, Oregon, for the hearing, is on the left. (Photograph courtesy of *Sun-Times Media*)

wanted to see U.S. Cellular Field, the new baseball stadium for the Chicago White Sox, so we drove past the ballpark.

At my aunt's house, we had a celebration with about fifty people, including some from out of town. Several reporters from the papers and TV also showed up. I walked around all night with a bottle of champagne. We stayed up very late, and I got very drunk—too drunk. We had fish and chicken and the family served me a plate of peach cobbler, which was a favorite of mine.

I slept well that night, and it was weird to wake up in a room without bars. It was sure much more comfortable sleeping in a nice bed rather than on a prison cot. At breakfast, I had real eggs, not powdered ones. It was very strange, but it didn't take me long to adjust. Life outside of a prison cell was easy to take.

In the following days, I didn't waste any time to put my life back together again as a free man. I went to various government offices to get the papers I needed such as my Social Security and state identification cards.

It was a joy to get reestablished with my family, and I went to visit my mother's and grandmother's graves at the Burr Oak Cemetery in Alsip, Illinois. I even started looking for work. Of course, I realized that I was only out on bond. The decision on my final status had yet to be made.

11.

Andrew Wilson's Affidavit

Andrew Wilson's affidavit, of which we were informed by the jailhouse lawyer, Philip W. McDowell, was important to me because it was additional proof, and ultimate proof, from the man who killed the McDonald's security guard that I was innocent.

As I wrote earlier, McDowell, a prisoner who helped inmates with legal issues, read stories about my case in the media, and on March 18, 2008, wrote the letter to Winston, informing him of an affidavit that Andrew Wilson had drawn up in which he admitted to the shooting and in which he swore I was innocent.

McDowell said he never received any instructions on whom to send the affidavit to, but he believed that Wilson did want it to go to someone in authority. In his affidavit, Wilson stated:

> *I, Andrew Wilson, hereby swear under penalty of perjury that no threats, promises or payments induced me to*

make or sign this affidavit, the statements below are both true and correct in substance and in fact:

1. *I am illiterate. I can neither read or write beyond a 3–4 grade level. As a result, I have solicited Philip McDowell to help me prepare this document. Mr. McDowell has previously aided me with other legal pleadings. My signature and initials below affirm that each paragraph of this affidavit has been read aloud and explained to me by Mr. McDowell. I further attest that although not in words I might choose Mr. McDowell has accurately restated and summarized here facts I have divulged to him relating a shooting I participated in January 11, 1982, at a McDonald's on 114th and Halsted in Chicago.*

2. *Although my true name is Andrew Wilson, I usually introduce myself prefer to be called, and am best known as "Gino," a long-time nickname.*

3. *I am incarcerated within the Illinois Department of Corrections. I am serving a life sentence that results from two convictions for first degree murder in connection with the February 09, 1982 shootings of Chicago Police Officers William Fahey and Richard O'Brien.*

4. *Although at two trials I insisted (through counsel) I had no involvement in the murders of Officers Fahey and O'Brien, I did in fact shoot both men. Jackie Wilson however (my brother) had nothing*

whatsoever to do with my actions that day nor did he or anyone else know the true reason I shot the officers. I told absolutely nobody because by doing so I would implicate myself in the shooting at McDonald's. This is because the weapon that Officer Fahey saw in my jacket was the revolver I had taken from the guard I shot in the chest January 11, 1982.

5. *I did not go to the McDonald's that night intending to shoot anyone, nor did I even plan on being inside. I was outside in the car talking to my friend Derrick Martin while my friends Ace (Edgar Hope) and "Nadia" (Nadine Smart) went inside the restaurant to get our food.*

6. *Parking near the front, about 20–30 feet from the door, Derrick and I could see very well inside the uncrowded McDonald's. The front part of the building was mostly glass and well lit. I had no trouble seeing Ace and Nadia at the counter.*

7. *After a few minutes passed, Derrick and I noticed Ace seemed upset and was arguing with a female in uniform behind the counter by the door. Alternately pointing to the menu-board, something in Nadia's hand and at the employee, Ace was shaking his head, frowning. Ace appeared to speak briefly with a man also behind the counter but resumed talking to the female.*

8. *Laughing at some animated reactions by other*

customers to Ace's antics, Derrick and I saw two armed men raise up from their table and started towards Ace and Nadia. I knew from being at the McDonald's several times before the guys were security guards. I had not seen them earlier and neither Ace or Nadia seemed to notice the men watching them, moving in their direction. I knew Ace had a warrant out for him (a robbery) so I decided to go into the restaurant, taking a single barrel, sawed-off pump action shotgun with me. The reason I stayed in the car.

9. Although I didn't know until later, Ace also was armed with a handgun, inside the McDonald's. Holding on to the shotgun through a hole in my pocket, I hid it under my coat and tried to get out of the car. However, I was so intently watching the two guards that my coat got caught in the door, jarring the shotgun from my hand. I dropped it on the parking lot pavement where it lay in plain view while I turned back to untangle my coat. Derrick stayed in the car, slipping behind the driver's wheel.

10. When I approached the glass door entrance of the McDonald's Ace saw my approach. He was at the first register to my left, partially turned toward the guard nearest to him. Almost right in front of the door stood the second guard.

11. I opened the door; the guard by Ace suddenly moved

forward. Reflexively, I brought the shotgun up and told the guard to "get back." At nearly the same time I fired a single shot, striking him in the left chest. Pumping another shell into the breach, I walked further into the restaurant. I stood near the center of the counter behind which the man Ace spoke to and two girls were hiding. Ignoring them, I looked for Nadia who I found crouched beside a nearby salad bar.

12. *I next saw Ace with a handgun, pointing it at the second guard who was now on the floor. Ace took the guy's gun from him so I walked over to the guard I'd shot who had slumped to the floor and took his weapon. Ace then said something to that guard, stood over him and shot him in the head. Ace, Nadia and I swiftly exited the McDonald's through the door I'd entered only moments earlier. The entire incident spanned 3–5 minutes.*

13. *Running towards it, I saw Derrick start the car. Ace got into the front seat, Nadia and I leapt into the back. We all yelled "Go!" "Go!" "Go!" to Derrick who drove south on Halsted. I told him to go to the Beauty Shop where I stayed. Derrick turned into the alley behind the shop and all of us went inside where Ace, Nadia and I changed clothes.*

14. *I gave Nadia a "Duke" sweatshirt and Ace a shirt and jeans (we were about the same size.) Ace had blood on*

his pants which along with all of our coats, I put into a trash bag. I stashed the bag and the shotgun in my room at the shop taking the guard's gun with me when I left. It was a fully loaded, .38 Caliber revolver.

15. We were at, in and out of the shop in 15–20 minutes. We drove west on 114th a half block and got on the freeway. We first went to 71st and King Drive to drop Nadia off then doubled back to go to our friend "Kojak's" house (Ronny), where we watched news reports about the incident. [Correcting the name "Ronny," Wilson, in pencil, inserted "Donny."]

16. That night, it was from news reports that we learned the man Ace shot survived. Telling everyone in the house he'd shot the man in the head at "point-blank" range, Ace brandished the gun he's taken, a .357 Magnum, and showed the guys what he did inside the McDonald's. I told him to quit talking about what happened even to other members of our gang, "Black Gangster Disciples." Derrick though kept asking Ace and I to see the guns we'd taken. Ace showed his off to everyone who asked. I on the other hand refused.

17. Over the next few days I got rid of the trash bag in which Nadia, Ace and I had put our clothes. For weeks I tried to catch the news everyday, watching for anything that police knew I was at the McDonald's that night. I was not at all bothered by the inaccurate

reporting [that] the incident was a thwarted robbery attempt, and the surviving guard a hero. Ace however always said the guard shouldn't be alive whenever newscasters spoke to him.

18. My identity as the second man at the McDonald's on January 11, 1982, was never exposed. Of the four who knew the truth, I always felt my secret was least safe with Derrick. Consequently, when police falsely accused and arrested Alton Logan, as Ace's accomplice, I put a gun to Derrick's head and threatened to blow his head off if he ever told what he knew. To similarly threaten Nadia, I unsuccessfully sought her out as well. Never again though did I ever see her. A couple of days later I fatally encountered Officers Fahey and O'Brien.

19. Even though police found the shotgun I used that night and found me in possession of the .38 of the guard I shot, never once was I questioned about the January 11, 1982, McDonald's shooting. That someone else was charged with what I'd done was not a good feeling. However, I thought the mistake might help Ace get off, and I never imagined Alton Logan would be convicted. And later, when I was sentenced to die, I admit I didn't care about anyone anymore nor had any interest whatsoever in the outcome of his or Ace's trial(s).

20. *On death row, I heard Ace and Alton Logan were convicted. Several times I contemplated coming forward but did not. My lawyers said my chances on appeal were good so I waited. We won, but again I was convicted. I became embittered by the life sentence and again expected the guy to be acquitted when I heard he and Ace got new trials.*

21. *When Alton Logan was convicted a second time of the shooting I'd done, I was again surprised, then shocked when unexpectedly meeting him personally in Pontiac prison in 1995. He asked me directly if I shot the McDonald's guard. Unnerved by the confrontation I answered that I had no idea what he was talking about. Because he was at the same prison I was, I sought and was placed in protective custody (P.C.) shortly after this meeting.*

    Were it not for my own appeals, and a resultant new trial, I may have sooner admitted my role in the McDonald's shooting. Nevertheless, in com-ing forward today, I hope finally to help ["clear"* is inserted here in pencil] *Alton Logan, someone whom I know is in fact innocent.*[35]

---

35. We explained two substantive corrections in the affidavit made in pencil by Andrew Wilson. He also made a few others that were very minor. I never saw Wilson's affidavit until Berl found it in 2015 while conducting research for our book. It was very moving to read the confession of the man who killed Wickliffe more than a quarter of a century earlier, and that he cleared me of any involve-ment. I read it many times, and each time I did, I got goose bumps.

Winston followed up on the letter by meeting with McDowell at the Danville Correctional Center where McDowell was doing time for murder.[36] They discussed the affidavit but McDowell could not find a copy until Winston left. McDowell later read it to Winston on the phone. As I indicated, the original that Wilson signed and had notarized in prison apparently was lost.

We deposed McDowell on March 17, 2010, when I hired the law firm, Loevy & Loevy, to file suit against Jon Burge, several detectives, and the City of Chicago, and he explained the circumstances that led Wilson to ask that the affidavit be created, and why he (McDowell) wrote to Winston, Judge Schreier, and several attorneys informing them of the affidavit's existence. Loevy & Loevy obtained a copy of the affidavit.

In his deposition, McDowell stated that Wilson, when he was in the Pontiac Correctional Center, received a letter from Richard S. Kling, the Chicago–Kent College of Law clinical law professor whom I mentioned earlier. Kling was representing Hope.

The letter asked him (Wilson), McDowell said, to confess to the McDonald's murder and to admit he committed the murder with me. McDowell said Wilson asked him to draft a letter telling Kling not to write him anymore, particularly about the McDonald's shooting.

---

36. McDowell, convicted of a fatal stabbing and sentenced to sixty years, was imprisoned in 1989 and also maintained he was innocent, stating that deputies beat him until he confessed.

In his own signed and notarized affidavit dated April 8, 2008, which was filed with Judge Schreier, McDowell stated: "At Andrew Wilson's request, I typed a negative reply to Mr. Kling and advised Mr. Kling future letters of this nature would be ignored. Never again did Andrew bring me another letter from Mr. Kling, nor anyone else requesting admissions to past offenses."

Wilson decided to draft his own affidavit. McDowell said that Wilson was almost illiterate and he (McDowell) "served as a jailhouse lawyer for Andrew Wilson around 1998–2000." McDowell met with Wilson on about fifty different occasions and prepared the affidavit between December 1999 and May 2000. McDowell said he saw Wilson sign the document and have it notarized by a prison official.

According to McDowell, Wilson confessed and tried to clear me because he really didn't like the fact that somebody else was incarcerated for "something that he [Wilson] had done." He wanted to "get rid of the stain of the conviction of Alton Logan."

McDowell said soon after he mailed his letter to several parties involved in my case, the story of the affidavit appeared in Chicago newspapers and a radio station also reported on it.

McDowell added that Kling represented him from 2002–07, and when he asked him about the letter he sent Wilson, Kling replied that he didn't want to talk about it.

I never had any dealings with Kling except for one brief meeting when I was in Stateville in September 1999. Kling was the court-appointed attorney for Hope, representing him in the shooting of Officer Doyle on the CTA bus that I discussed in

Chapter 2. The guards told me there were lawyers waiting to talk to me in the visitors' lounge. I thought it was Erica Reddick.

The "attorneys" turned out to be two of Kling's law students along with an investigator, Jonathan Lyon, who took notes. The students asked me several questions. I didn't like it at all. I stopped the interview, angrily telling them, "Don't you know I have a lawyer and that I have to ask her about being questioned by you?" One student left and returned with Kling, who ended the meeting. He said I could go back to my cell.

Berl interviewed Kling twice on several issues by telephone. Regarding the students, Kling said he didn't know why his students would interview me without my lawyer present. He added, "But, if I stopped it, it was because they should not interview anyone who is represented by counsel." Of course, this doesn't explain why the students came to see me in the first place. Kling had to be involved in the planning process; the students didn't just suddenly decide to visit me in prison on their own.

I think Kling wanted information from me to help clear Hope even though there was no question as to Hope's guilt in participating in the murder of Wickliffe and in attempting to kill Thompson. After all, it was Hope who tried to help me from the beginning by telling his attorney, Marc Miller, one month after my arrest to notify my lawyer that I was innocent. He basically confessed by making that request of Miller. Further, there were several other witnesses who, through the years, swore in affidavits that Hope and/or Wilson confessed to them as having killed Wickliffe.

It wasn't long before Winston learned of the meeting with the students, and he was livid. He wrote Kling a letter stating that he was "surprised" that his "agents" had visited me without checking with Winston's office. Winston asked for all the notes and wrote that neither Kling nor his students were ever to meet with me again. Also, Winston made a point of stating that he was holding Kling responsible for the meeting with me and not the students.

Kling responded angrily, writing he was "really tired" of Winston's "arrogant condescending attitude," adding he would send along any notes the students might have taken. He concluded the letter with the following: "It appears that you have something up a portion of your anatomy that apparently is interfering with your ability to think clearly and function professionally and courteously."

Winston, being the gentleman that he is, wrote back that while his and Kling's interests were "in many respects conflicting, several areas of common concern exist . . . and I hope we can work together against the State in those areas."

Regarding McDowell's deposition, Kling said that what McDowell alleged wasn't true, that McDowell was a "manipulative lying nut."

"I never did either of those two things [ask Wilson to confess and implicate me]," said Kling. "I represented Philip for a while until he started accusing me, a couple of judges, the . . . prosecutor and [stated that] everyone is essentially conspiring to make sure he stayed in." Asked if he wrote any kind of letter to Wilson, Kling said, "No, not that I recall. I may have written him a letter to ask if I could see him in the penitentiary. I just don't remember. But I certainly didn't write him a letter saying I wanted [him] to confess." Kling acknowledged that he went to see Wilson in prison. Wilson refused to meet with him.

In a deposition with Loevy & Loevy, Kling was asked if in his investigation of the case, "Alton Logan was also implicated," and he responded, "Yes." When Berl asked Kling specifically what that evidence was, he said, "I don't have the slightest idea."

In his exchange of letters with McDowell between 2015 and 2017 when McDowell was in the Dixon Correctional Center in Dixon, Illinois, Berl asked McDowell for a copy of the letter that he said Kling sent Wilson. McDowell refused, primarily because he was angry with me for not thanking him for coming forward with the information about Wilson's affidavit.

To be frank, so much was happening in my case I really didn't think about it. I was preoccupied with all the issues I faced as we continued our fight in court. He's right, though. I should have thanked him. All I can say is that I am very sorry about that. It was an unintended oversight, and I regret it.

When McDowell didn't respond to one of Berl's last letters, Berl wrote him again, stating he was prepared to travel from Michigan and visit McDowell in Dixon to talk with him face-to-face about the letter. McDowell answered that his attorneys advised him not to meet with anyone. He gave Berl the names of his attorneys (Jennifer Blagg and Lauren Kaeseberg) and their phone numbers in Chicago. Berl called them several times. Neither Blagg nor Kaeseberg called back.

Kling's involvement with my case arose again on January 28, 2010, when my lawyers from Loevy & Loevy deposed Jackie Wilson, Andrew Wilson's brother. Jackie Wilson, whom Kling had represented twice in previous years, was asked by my attorneys about an affidavit that he signed on August 24, 2000, which contained the following sentence: "Alton Logan . . . told me that he used the shotgun to kill Lloyd Wickliffe." The affidavit was drafted by Kling on behalf of Hope.

Jackie Wilson[37] stated in the deposition he didn't know how that sentence got into the affidavit, that when he signed it, he hadn't read it carefully. He said several times in the deposition that I was innocent. He said he told Winston:

"Look, call me to court, and I will testify in open court that this statement is not true, because it was not . . . I don't know how it wound up there." In addition, Wilson said that he told Kling I was innocent.

Berl also asked Kling about the affidavit containing the sentence that I told Wilson that I fired the shotgun. During one of the two phone interviews, Kling said he didn't prepare the affidavit, asking, "What does the affidavit say?" Berl emailed

---

37. As of April 2017, Jackie Wilson was in the Stateville Correctional Center. He was fifty-six. Berl wrote to him, asking how he believed the respective sentence got into his affidavit. Wilson was represented by Loevy & Loevy, which responded to Berl that it preferred Wilson didn't get involved in a discussion of the affidavit. I knew Jackie Wilson, but we weren't friends. We spoke cordially when we ran into each other at different prisons. Imprisoned in 1983, he is not eligible for parole.

the relevant part of the affidavit to Kling, who responded in an email with the following statement:

"I have no memory of the affidavit or of any connection to Jackie. If I indeed prepared the affidavit with that sentence, then Jackie must have told me that or I would never have included it."

Kling was deposed on November 29, 2010, by Loevy & Loevy, and he was shown the affidavit in question. He responded: "This appears to be an affidavit of—oh, I remember this. This is the affidavit that we—that Mr. Wilson signed that I then filed in Edgar Hope's McDonald's case."

In that deposition, he also answered, "Yes," when asked whether Jackie Wilson told him that I used the shotgun to kill Lloyd Wickliffe.

In his second interview with Berl, Kling said he probably remembered the affidavit during his deposition—which, he said, he also didn't remember—because Loevy & Loevy showed him the affidavit, and he recognized it. He said he had no "independent recollection" of the affidavit.

Interestingly, despite the court hearings on the Kunz–Coventry affidavit and the ruling by Judge Schreier, Kling, two years after I was set free, still maintained in the deposition that Hope never waived his lawyer-client privilege to confidentiality. Specifically, Kling said:

"Marc Miller should be throttled for having waived the privilege without Edgar Hope's permission. Edgar Hope never gave him (Miller) permission to waive the privilege. Edgar Hope continued to maintain that anything he said was privileged."

In addition, he believed that Hope was innocent, stating, "That one of the perpetrators was Andrew Wilson, I think, is indisputable. Who the other one was, our only position was it's not Edgar Hope."

As I stated earlier, there is no doubt that Hope was Andrew Wilson's accomplice. If he was not with Andrew Wilson at the time of the shooting in McDonald's, he obviously couldn't have told Marc Miller that I was innocent. He stressed to Miller that his only partner in the crimes he committed was Andrew Wilson, and the two had a long history together.

Kling said something else that fascinated me about the Kunz–Coventry affidavit. Like Barbara Kamm, who said she heard rumors about some documents that were locked up that might help me, Kling said he and members of the Public Defender's Office knew about the Kunz–Coventry affidavit even before my first trial in 1983. He couldn't remember who had told him about the document.

"Internally, the whole family knew about it," Kling said. "When I say the family, the Homicide Task Force." He said he never saw the actual affidavit; he learned of its content "a couple of years ago [in 2008]."[38]

He agreed with the characterization made during a deposition that he didn't speak up because since he "didn't have a dog in the fight, he didn't want to get involved."

In the deposition, he also concurred with Coventry that

---

38. Kling was a member of the Public Defender's Office from 1976–81. He was part of the department's Special Homicide Task Force.

if anyone had approached the prosecutors with information that they had an affidavit that vouched for my innocence, they would have ignored it because such a revelation could have jeopardized their cases against Wilson and Hope.

Asked what he would have done had he been in a position like Coventry's and Kunz's, Kling replied:

"The identical approach. I would have lost a lot of sleep. I would have talked to a psychologist or talked to colleagues, and I would have kept my mouth shut because I think under the rules of professional responsibility then and now, we have an absolute obligation to do that [remain silent]."

We deposed Winston for the civil suit I would file against the city (I discuss it in the next chapter), and he was asked about Kling and his relationship to Jackie Wilson. A portion of what Winston said follows:

Q. Did you take issue with any part of the process with which Richard Kling obtained this statement from Jackie Wilson that tended to inculpate Mr. Logan?

A. I believe I complained to Professor Kling that that's not what . . . Jackie was telling me, and I probably communicated with him that Jackie said he didn't notice that in his statement. I was certainly very upset because I—it would seem to me I would see Jackie and he'd . . . say things helpful to us and then he's always be signing off for Kling that said the opposite. I think he ended up doing an affidavit too.

Q. Did you think that Kling had something to do with getting Jackie to flip on you?[39]

A. Yes.

Q. And did you think there was anything improper about what Kling was doing in trying to get statements out of Jackie or any other witness?

A. Well, he has a right to try and get statements. I don't think I want to say anything more than that.

When pressed, Winston refused to speculate, stating, "I was not there when Kling interviewed witnesses and was not present. I don't think I can go beyond what I said."

Another thing that bothered me was that the statement about me allegedly telling Wilson that I fired the shotgun ended up in the media. I didn't need such bad publicity, especially since it wasn't true.

As a matter of fact, Jackie Wilson didn't like the media attention either because, Winston pointed out in his deposition, the press coverage told "the gang"—other prisoners—that Wilson was talking with lawyers and/or authorities As a result, Wilson said he was being threatened in prison.

One more point: I was preparing for a visit from my

---

39. In interviews with Berl, Winston said the lawyers did not mean him. Instead, Winston said, they meant Kling tried to get Jackie Wilson to flip on me.

brother, Eugene, a few days after the meeting with the law students, when a guard informed me I was to be taken to seg. I asked why. The guard said he didn't know. I objected, stating that I was going to see my brother unless someone gave me a reason for being ordered to solitary. The guard left and it wasn't long before a lieutenant followed by a captain came to my cell. I said I wanted answers. The two told me I was considered a "security threat." I complained, in writing, all the way up to the warden. My protests were ignored. Someone speculated that the order "to seg me" came from prison authorities "higher up" in Springfield, Illinois.

In solitary, I noticed the guards had cleared all the cells on the floor. I was locked in a cell on one side and Jackie Wilson on the other. I had never seen anything like that. Jackie Wilson was in solitary for about two months; I was kept for six before I was returned to the general population. To this day, I never learned how or why this happened.[40]

All that I have written about was in the past. The time had come for me to focus on the future, specifically, on the September 4, 2008 court hearing that would decide my fate. I prayed that finally I would be a free man again. My hopes and dreams were in the hands of Judge Schreier.

---

40. Berl asked for the records on this incident from the Illinois Department of Corrections (IDOC) under the Freedom of Information Act (FOIA). The freedom of information officer, Lisa Weitekamp, sent him an email on May 10, 2016, stating that her office was unable to locate any records "that respond to [the] request."

12.

Exoneration, Innocence Certificate, Civil Suit

We had three procedural court appearances in May, July, and August before my court date on September 4, 2008, in front of Judge Schreier.

I was out of prison, true. It had been a long wait. I had lots of anxiety. Who knew what would or could happen, what the state would do? Would I go through all of this again?

As the September date approached, I worried a lot. Two witnesses, Dawson and Thompson, who said I did it, were still around.

It was time for the decision. Apprising the judge that the state conducted a comprehensive review of all the evidence, and that it wouldn't be able to meet its burden of proof to prove me guilty, Assistant Illinois Attorney General Richard D. Schwind said:

Judge, as you correctly stated for the record today the People are going to inform the Court as to whether or not they are going to continue to pursue the prosecution of Mr. Logan. The Attorney General's Office was undergoing a systematic and thorough review of the evidence in that case. We have concluded that thorough review and completed the investigation, talked to witnesses, and the conclusion of that is we would be unable to meet our burden of proof in this matter, and in the interests of justice the most appropriate decision at this time would be to dismiss all charges against Mr. Logan.

Judge Schreier replied:

A few words, if I may. Based on the evidence adduced at the post-conviction hearing and the complete record of the case, I believe Attorney General [Lisa] Madigan and her assistants did the right thing in dismissing this indictment and I commend her office for this decision.

The judge continued, addressing me directly:

From all that I heard, Mr. Logan, it appears you did not commit this murder, and your conviction and twenty-six-year incarceration is most regrettable. Most regrettable. We know the American justice system is imperfect, but that must have been little consolation for you during the many years behind bars. You have, to borrow a phrase, endured a season in purgatory. But now to paraphrase another expression, your long personal nightmare is over. Hopefully, you will have a long life as a free man.

Finally, a wrong had been righted. I didn't have to look over my shoulder anymore. Of course, I was pissed, and even more so when I learned about all the things the police and prosecutors did to have me convicted.

I thought back to the time I was arrested on February 7, 1982, and the fact that just six days later police matched a shell found at McDonald's to a shotgun confiscated while seeking Wilson for the murder of two police officers. Not only didn't the police follow up on this evidence, they hid it from my lawyers. Again, this happened just six days after I was locked up for the crime. How my life would have been different if the cops and the "officers of the court" had done their jobs honestly.

I might add that even after we finally got the report on the ballistics tests matching the gun to the shell casing, Judge Bailey refused to admit the evidence, stating this was not a trial for Andrew Wilson. Of course it wasn't. He seemed to forget and ignore the fact that we were trying to prove my innocence.

As I wrote earlier, there was no use reliving the past. I needed to move on. I hired the Chicago law firm of Loevy &

Loevy to petition the court to grant me what was called a certificate of innocence. Yes, I was exonerated, but it was still very difficult to explain to people what happened to me. I wanted a paper that said I was innocent.

The State of Illinois, on September 22, 2008, about five months before I filed for this certificate, passed legislation providing a process by which the wrongfully convicted could apply for such a certificate. This document served the cause of justice, and with the certificate, I would be eligible for help in finding a job, resume preparation, and other employment assistance.

In many states, exonerees receive no help whatsoever after they are freed. Ironically, ex-convicts—those who were guilty—were provided help in finding jobs and social welfare assistance.

Under the new Illinois law, I was able to petition the Circuit Court for the certificate that I could present to the Illinois Court of Claims.[41] Most importantly, I could receive compensation,[42] which is calculated on the number of years the petitioner was in prison. Compensation was capped at fourteen years. For me, that meant I could receive $199,150, or an average of $7,659.61 per year for the twenty-six years I was imprisoned.

My petition was filed by Loevy & Loevy on January 27, 2009, and we had a one-day hearing before Cook County

---

41. The legislation establishing a certificate of innocence was vetoed by Illinois Gov. Rod Blagojevich. The veto was overridden and the act became law without the governor's signature.

42. As of 2017, the federal government, thirty-two states, and Washington, D.C., offered some compensation for exonerees. The compensation ranged from $5,000 per year in prison in Wisconsin to $83,000 annually in Texas. Eighteen states didn't provide any compensation. Source: Innocence Project (New York) website.

Circuit Court Judge Paul Biebel, Jr. The Loevy petition on my behalf stated:

> Every wrongful conviction is tragic and heartbreaking in its own right, but the horrors of Mr. Logan's ordeal were compounded by a unique circumstance: All through the decades that Mr. Logan languished behind bars, the identity of the real culprit was known to multiple officers of the court. Despite knowing the truth about who really committed this crime, these lawyers were duty-bound to stand by silently even as Mr. Logan fruitlessly pressed his claims of innocence over the years in the courts.
>
> In this way, the system failed Mr. Logan's case. The actual killer (the late Andrew Wilson) escaped justice; meanwhile, Mr. Logan unnecessarily wasted more than a quarter of a century behind bars. And while Mr. Wilson's attorneys may well have genuinely believed that they had ethical grounds to withhold the truth until after Mr. Wilson's death, the impact of their decision is very real. Mr. Logan lost nearly half of his life rotting in prison for a crime he did not commit.

The Loevy attorneys got it right when they wrote in my petition that "he [meaning me] has suffered immeasurably in an environment that can only be described as 'hell on earth.'"

The petition added that I was "fortunate enough" to get a job with the Metropolitan Pier and Exposition Authority, loading and unloading trucks, "but the work is not steady enough and there are not enough hours."

We said in the brief that my employment options "proved very limited having lost 26 of the most productive years of his [my] life." We pointed out that I tried very hard to find permanent employment. Unfortunately, despite my efforts, I wasn't successful.

On April 17, 2009, about a year after my release and about three months after our hearing, I received a certificate of innocence from Judge Biebel.

We sent the document to the Court of Claims and my check for $199,150 arrived about a week later. The Attorney General's Office didn't oppose the granting of the certificate.

In an interview regarding the certificate on radio station WBEZ, I broke down and said, "It (the certificate) means a lot to me. I don't have that feeling in my back anymore because they could take it back. They could do this, they could do that. Now, I know they can't do anything. That's a whole lift off my back."

In my next legal action, we filed a federal civil rights suit in the U.S. District Court Northern District of Illinois, Eastern Division on September 3, 2009 charging that I was the victim of a wrongful conviction resulting from misconduct by the City of Chicago, Jon Burge, and several detectives.

Financially, I was basically trying to stay alive. I was

living off the generosity of my family. I hoped that a settlement would put me back on my feet and ease the burden on my family. I believed the government owed me something, although regardless of what I might win in court, it would never make up for the years I lost.

In seeking damages, the suit charged that the police conspired to build a false case against me irrespective of my guilt or innocence. Besides Burge, the detectives named were: George Basile, Fred Hill, Thomas McKenna, Anthony Katalinic, James Pienta, and Joseph Digiacomo.

In the suit, we charged that "the defendants unjustly singled out the Plaintiff, who had already been accused of the crime, and then endeavored to stretch and manipulate the facts and the evidence to fit the false hypothesis that he was guilty."

Loevy Attorney Russell Ainsworth listed violations the detectives committed in framing me for the McDonald's murder. These included:

- Failing to disclose . . . exculpatory evidence.
- Manufacturing evidence to falsely implicate me.
- Hiding testimony from witnesses who identified Andrew Wilson as the murderer.
- Disregarding and/or destroying exculpatory evidence.
- Systematically secreting discoverable information.
- Working to secure false convictions through profoundly flawed investigations.

The suit said that in serving more than twenty-six years "behind bars, Logan was wrongfully deprived of nearly half of his life . . . stripped of the various pleasures of [the] basic human experience which all free people enjoy as a matter of right." That said it about as accurately as possible.

In the suit we pointed out that numerous police reports and other records were missing and we cited the following major facts:

- There was never any physical evidence tying me to the crime. Police didn't find any fingerprints, DNA, nor was there any incriminating evidence of any kind discovered in my possession. As a matter of fact, the only physical evidence the prosecutors had implicated Edgar Hope and Andrew Wilson.

- When Lt. Burge arrested Andrew Wilson for the murder of Officers Fahey and O'Brien, Wilson was in possession of a .38 caliber revolver he had stolen from Lloyd Wickliffe, and Burge failed to reveal this exculpatory evidence when I was tried. The other defendants named in our suit also knew of the recovery of this weapon.

- Detective Thomas Bennett who, as I mentioned earlier, was a member of the investigative team that worked on my case, disclosed under oath that Burge bragged about me being wrongfully convicted and that the real murderer was Wilson.[43]

- The defendants fabricated evidence, which included manipulating witnesses, especially Anthonette Dawson and Charles Trent. We charged that the police engaged in "improper suggestiveness and outright coercion."
- The defendants never revealed that one witness, Gail Hilliard, positively identified Wilson as the shooter and that she said I wasn't the one who fired the shotgun.
- The detectives never revealed that Donald G. White, to whose home Wilson and Hope went after the McDonald's murder, told police that the two had confessed to him that they killed the security guard at McDonald's.

We listed other illegal actions taken by the police, many of which my attorneys cited in appeals for some twenty-five years—a quarter of a century. The claims we made were all

---

43. Berl talked briefly to Detective Bennett on the telephone in June 2016, and asked him if he ever told anyone that his friend, fellow Detective Charles R. Grunhard (cited in Chapter 8) said that Burge told him (Grunhard) that I was innocent. This incident happened in the late 1980s, only a few years after my first conviction in 1983. Bennett said he did not share the information with anyone because he didn't know if it was true. Grunhard, terminally ill, had no reason to lie, especially to his friend. It seems that Bennett should have told someone. If he couldn't tell police supervisors, at least, he could have alerted prosecutors, and maybe it would have forced them to take another look at my case. Or, he might have spoken—even secretly—to my attorneys.

rejected by several appellate courts. As a matter of fact, Jack Rimland, my attorney in the first trial, cited more than forty issues in trying to win a new trial for me after my conviction in 1983. Regrettably, he was unsuccessful.

Overall, the suit said the defendants "withheld valuable information that would have prevented Logan from ever being convicted at trial."

I want to point out the defendants refused to answer many questions when they were deposed. Instead, they invoked the Fifth Amendment, which provides constitutional protection against self-incrimination.

We asked for a jury trial, and in preparation, my lawyers deposed several people who would be important for our case. I am including brief sections of some of these depositions as they relate to my innocence. The records paint a stark picture of the blatant violations by the police in framing me for the McDonald's murder.

In a deposition dated July 13, 2010, Donald White stated that he was arrested and interrogated about the murders of Fahey and O'Brien. He denied being involved—which he wasn't.

He was also questioned about the McDonald's murder and shown a photograph of me. The cops asked him to identify me. He swore in his deposition:

"I had never seen or heard of this guy before. The detectives did not want to hear it. They said that I better identify this person they called Logan in the McDonald's murder or they would charge me with a rape case."

White said he told the cops that Edgar "Ace" Hope had committed the murder/robbery with Andrew "Gino" Wilson. He described how Hope and Wilson came to his house after the shooting and showed off the guns they had stolen from the Cook County sheriff's deputies. He also said in his deposition that he met with the Wilson brothers to discuss how to break Edgar Hope out of the hospital where he was recuperating from a gunshot wound in his side suffered during the shootout in which Hope killed Officer Doyle on the CTA bus. Hope had threatened to confess to all the murders and robberies they had committed if his friends didn't try to free him.

White insisted that he didn't know me. He said the cops refused to accept his answer and continually beat him. At one point, White said that Burge admitted knowing that "Andrew [Wilson] was present [at McDonald's], but that he wanted Logan."

White said, ultimately, he couldn't take the beatings anymore, and "I gave in and identified his photograph as being involved in the McDonald's case."

White concluded his deposition, stating: "I only implicated Alton Logan in the McDonald's case when I was coerced into doing so. All these years, I have known that he was innocent and have regretted giving in to the pressure that the police put on me."

My attorney, Jon Loevy, also deposed Jackie Wilson on January 28, 2010, in the Stateville Correctional Center where

Wilson was doing time for the murders of the two Chicago police officers.

Like White, Jackie Wilson said he was asked "a thousand questions" regarding the McDonald's murder, and he told detectives I wasn't involved. He repeatedly said I was innocent. The following is a short excerpt from his deposition:

Q. You have no knowledge of Alton Logan being involved in that crime [McDonald's], correct?

A. I know for a fact that he wasn't there.

Q. It is your belief that Alton Logan is innocent.

A. I know he is.

Q. How is that [you know Alton Logan wasn't involved]?

A. Because my brother [Andrew Wilson] told me . . .

He repeated the fact that I wasn't involved in the shooting at McDonald's several times in his deposition, which runs more than 200 pages.

In summary, we said, "In serving more than twenty-six years behind bars . . . He missed out on the ability to share holidays, births, funerals, and other life events with loved ones, and the fundamental freedom to live one's life as an autonomous human being."

Just before we were to begin the trial, on December 3,

I am walking out of court for the last time September 4, 2008, with Harold
Winston, the lead attorney on my public defender legal team, and Susan Smith,
assistant public defender. (Photograph courtesy of *Sun-Times Media*)

2012, we settled out of court for damages totaling $10.25
million,[44] a little more than three years after I filed the suit and
thirty years after I was arrested. The Chicago City Council
approved payment on January 17, 2013.

In interviews, Jon Loevy said the settlement was long
overdue, "for a man who is still struggling with the transition
nearly five years after his release from prison.

> Mr. Logan lost twenty-six years of his life. He went to
> prison in his twenties. He came out in his fifties. No

---

44. After I paid off all the lawyers' fees for twenty-six years, paid the commission on
the settlement plus took care of loans and other financial obligations incurred by
the family during the years of my imprisonment, I was left with about $5 million.

Harold Winston, the lead attorney on my public defender legal team, holds up my certificate of innocence, which validated my exoneration, at a press conference April 17, 2009, in the law offices of Loevy & Loevy, which, on my behalf, filed a civil rights suit against the City of Chicago. (Photograph courtesy of *Sun-Times Media*)

amount of money can compensate a man for everything [he lost] under those circumstances. It's hard to make a life when you've lost so much. He's applied for hundreds of jobs. When they find out about the hole in his resume, it makes it very hard. His case is an example of a sad truth: Sometimes the wrong guy gets convicted of a crime. Fortunately, in this instance, the truth came out.

Jon Loevy hit the nail on the head. Regarding the money, some imply that I shouldn't complain because I received a good settlement to which I respond:

They don't even know what I lost. They have no idea what

prison is like. They can't even imagine what it does to people. The money couldn't pay for the years I spent in prison. There is only one thing I wanted and that was the life that was taken from me. That I couldn't get. I could never be paid off. No amount of money could make up for what I endured. What the money did was bring me a measure of security because it allowed me to live my life in a comfortable manner.

I also want to emphasize that even though the city paid this money, it wasn't an admission of guilt. No one apologized, something I wanted someone in power to do.

Reporters asked Richard Daley, the state's attorney, whether he would offer an apology. He responded that he couldn't recall the case. "You know how many cases we had in the state's attorney's office?" he asked rhetorically.

It is inconceivable that Daley didn't remember my case, or that he didn't know it inside-out. His office prosecuted me for some twenty years before the case was turned over to the Attorney General's Office. At the time of my exoneration, I received massive publicity in Chicago, and was covered on *60 Minutes* and by the media throughout the country. I am confident Daley knew my case and knew it well.

As much as I wanted the apology, I knew Daley and the others involved would never offer one.

13.

Proposed Changes
in Ethics Code

Berl and I are not lawyers. We appreciate the complexity of issues faced by attorneys. Nevertheless, we want to make some suggestions on amending the lawyers' code of ethics as it relates to lawyer-client confidentiality.

We know that each of our recommendations will prompt criticism, particularly from strict constructionists. They will always find a reason to maintain the status quo. But change is necessary to prevent someone else from suffering the consequences that I endured.

I would guess that my case was unique. Judge Schreier said at my hearings, this was the most unusual case that he ever presided over.

In the research we conducted to write this book, we couldn't find even one case in which a lawyer used the exceptions provided for in Massachusetts and Alaska.

We are really talking about a change for a confluence of

circumstances that is extremely rare. Berl could only find one other similar case that unfolded almost exactly when mine did, and was almost identical. Tragically, it had the opposite result: the innocent person, as of April 2017, was still in prison.

In 1986 in Fayetteville, North Carolina, Lee Wayne Hunt was convicted, along with a co-defendant, Jerry Dale Cashwell, of the 1984 murders of a couple, Roland and Lisa Matthews. Hunt and Cashwell were each given two life sentences. In 2002, Cashwell committed suicide, and after his death, his lawyer, Staples Hughes, an appellate public defender in North Carolina, came forward to testify that Cashwell admitted to him in 1985 that Hunt was innocent, that he (Cashwell) had acted alone.

Like my case, the story was aired on *60 Minutes*. In statements similar to those made by Kunz and Coventry, Hughes said in the segment the circumstances "bothered" him, adding he regretted that "there wasn't anything I could do about it."

He decided to break his silence after Cashwell died because, he said, "It seemed . . . at that point ethically permissible and morally imperative that [I] spill the beans."

As he prepared to testify, he was cautioned by Cumberland County Superior Court Judge Jack A. Thompson not to do so. "If you testify," Judge Thompson is quoted in *The New York Times* as warning Hughes, "I will be compelled to report you to the state bar. Do you understand that?"

Hughes understood; he wasn't dissuaded. At a hearing

in 2007, Hughes ignored the judge's admonition. The judge refused to accept Hughes's testimony, ruling that Hughes was guilty of professional misconduct, and reported him to the state bar for violating the state's legal code of ethics. The North Carolina State Bar wouldn't discuss the disposition of the case with Berl. However, stories in the media reported that the bar dismissed the complaint in January 2008.

Judge Thompson also rejected motions that new evidence warranted a new trial for Hunt. His decision was upheld by the state's appeals court and, without giving any reasons, the North Carolina Supreme Court in January 2008 refused to hear the case, letting the lower court ruling stand.

Regarding the legal proceedings, Richard Rosen, a retired University of North Carolina School of Law professor and one of Hunt's attorneys, was quoted in the local media as saying, "I think as a whole, the judicial system of North Carolina should be ashamed of their treatment of this case from top to bottom."

Rosen told us he was aware of my exoneration and "happy [for me] and that there were people who were more interested in justice than a conviction." But he was "frustrated" that the same was not true in Hunt's case.

Hughes, reflecting on the situation, said in a story in *The New York Times:* "The only consequence for me is the bitterness and anger I feel over Mr. Hunt. I go home, have a glass of wine, work in the yard. And, there's a guy sitting in a prison camp two counties away, and my feeling is he's going to be there the rest of his life."

Hughes appeared on *60 Minutes* in November 2007, and described how he felt when Cashwell told him Hunt was innocent.

"It was sort of one of those moments that stops you completely still. You know, my client's saying, 'Not only did I kill two people, but these other folks didn't have anything to do with it. The state's case is a lie. It's a fabrication.'"

Asked by Correspondent Steve Kroft if he tried to convince Cashwell to confess to authorities, Hughes said, "No. I'm his lawyer. It wasn't in his interest to have that known to all. He was facing the death penalty. It wasn't theoretical."

Did the circumstances bother him? "It bothered me most when Mr. Hunt was being tried," Hughes replied. "And it's bothered me ever since. There wasn't anything I could do about it. But I knew they were trying a guy who didn't do it."

Hughes's arguments for remaining silent were almost identical to those of Coventry and Kunz.

In April 2017, Berl checked on the status of the case. Two of Hunt's other attorneys, Kenneth S. Broun, also a retired University of North Carolina School of Law professor, and Mary Pollard of Prisoner Legal Services, told him they were appealing a federal magistrate's denial for a new hearing. The appeal process would be a long one, they said, while expressing concern about Hunt's health. Hunt, who turned fifty-eight in June 2017, remained in the Mountain View Correctional Institution in Spruce Pine, North Carolina.

Incarcerated in October 1986, he already had spent more than thirty years in prison.[45]

Thus, Coventry was right when he told us: (a) the system wouldn't have accepted his testimony, and (b) I was lucky to have had Judge Schreier, who Coventry described as one of the few honorable judges in the system, hear my case.

Although situations like mine and Hunt's are extremely rare, ethical standards should be designed to protect the life of the innocent even if the respective code may apply to only a few people. We can think of no substantive reason why the code shouldn't be changed.

Undoubtedly, the absolutists will raise the "slippery slope" argument, i.e. if we change the code for cases like mine, what's next? Well, let's worry about the "what's next" when another issue raises questions about ethical requirements.

Meanwhile, let's put aside "how many angels can sit on the head of a pin" arguments and use a little common sense. As I sat in court all those years, I couldn't believe that adults with advanced degrees would engage in debates that would prompt ridicule from ten-year-olds. Prosecutors, defense lawyers, and judges would argue over minute, meaningless, and,

---

45. The only forensic evidence against Lee Wayne Hunt were bullet fragments found at the murder scene that were compared to a box of bullets belonging to Hunt. Used by the FBI for some forty years, bullet lead analysis, as it was called, involved examining the chemical makeup of a bullet and matching it to other bullets—in this case. Hunt's bullets—manufactured in the same factory. This analysis, discredited by many experts and called "junk science" by some, was discarded by the FBI in 2005.

yes, asinine issues, while people like me, whose lives were in their hands, had to sit helplessly by, powerless to do anything about it. That's a broader issue, of course, that I'm not prepared or qualified to deal with. However, I think I have a special and personal perspective on the lawyer-client confidentiality issue as it relates to changing the ethics code to permit innocent people wasting away in prison for life or on death row to go free.

I understand why Coventry, Kunz, Miller, and Lyon remained silent. I understand they "were only following the rules." Their obedience to the rules cost me dearly. I also know, firsthand, that the code is wrong, unjust, misguided, and needs to be changed.

We propose that the states work with the American Bar Association (ABA) to amend the lawyer-client confidentiality section to permit lawyers to compromise confidentiality when it might lead to an innocent person being exonerated.

We believe that the confidentiality requirement should be waived immediately when the client who gave an attorney confidential information dies. Coventry said that suggestion didn't seem "unreasonable" and might be adopted with a provision that the release of the confidential information after a client's death should not require a waiver from the client.

Winston recommended in a 2009 article[46] that the Illinois Rule of Professional Conduct 1.6 be amended to permit lawyers

46. "Learning from Alton Logan," *DePaul (University) Journal for Social Justice,* (Spring 2009) 173.

in situations like the one faced by Coventry and Kunz to provide the necessary information to save innocent individuals.

He planned to propose adoption of a stipulation that the information being released under a lawyer-client confidentiality relationship couldn't be used directly against the client in future legal proceedings. He said that such a change would help the cause of justice. Barbara Kamm agreed with Winston's proposal, stating that she would have "no problem" with that kind of amendment, adding it would have to be carefully drafted to assure the information provided is credible. This seems similar to provisions that permit prosecutors to grant immunity to witnesses for their testimony.

Another change that should be considered is to allow a breach of confidentiality when a lawyer's client faces other charges of similar severity and wouldn't be harmed by the respective information. In my case, Andrew Wilson already faced capital charges for the murder of two police officers. The information that he also killed Wickliffe, the security guard at McDonald's, hardly would have put him in more jeopardy.

As Berl indicates in his introduction, Andrea Lyon, dean of the Valparaiso Law School who notarized the affidavit, suggested a change that might find acceptance even among absolutists.

She proposed the equivalent of "in camera inspection" in which a judge reviews sensitive material in chambers to decide whether materials and information requested in a subpoena should be turned over.

Perhaps, she said, a "special master or ethics guru or czar" might be established who can be asked for special dispensations to reveal information in cases like mine. With that kind of procedure, she said, someone would be deciding the issue who wasn't a lawyer for opposing parties. If this mechanism had existed in my case, she speculated, the lawyers might have been able to break their silence.

Such a system might even involve a panel of, let's say, about five judges that makes a decision on the confidential evidence in secret and that decision could be binding, freeing the wrongly accused immediately. If this were done behind closed doors, no one would be harmed, including the individual who revealed the information to his/her attorney.

The major point in recommending changes in the ethics code is that we are talking about saving lives. The lawyers involved in my case—Coventry, Kunz, and Lyon—made a distinction between a death sentence and life imprisonment. Let me state clearly: they were totally wrong. To repeat, a life sentence is a death sentence. They have no idea what it's like to sit in prison, let alone sit in prison while innocent. It is, in a word, indescribable.

Telling us he was inspired by my case, Patrick T. Santos, a California attorney, published a comprehensive analysis[47] on

---

47. "Why the ABA Should Permit Lawyers to Use Their Get-Out-Of-Jail Free Card: A Theoretical and Empirical Analysis," *University of La Verne College of Law (La Verne, California) Review Journal*, 2009.

attorney-client confidentiality in which he captured the central issue: Life.

Advocating for the adoption of a narrow wrongful-conviction exception, Santos said the essence of the argument is, "grounded in the fundamental notion that an individual's physical liberty outweighs client candor."

He pointed out the ABA already had broadened its model rules to include exceptions that permit lawyers to reveal client information where an attorney "reasonably believes it necessary to prevent reasonably certain death or substantial bodily harm." He explained, "[T]he rationale behind the new rule is simple: The value of human life and bodily integrity trumps keeping client confidences."

He further argued that the justifications for a new wrongful-conviction exception to client confidentiality had already been supplied by the ABA. He said, "[T]he interests that confidentiality preserve . . . seem less important when juxtaposed with another human good—such as when life itself is at stake."

Kunz opposed any changes, stating he couldn't accept a provision that allowed him to reveal what his client had discussed with him in secret. He said if his client knew he (Kunz) could reveal the information, the client wouldn't be candid. Also, Kunz said an exception to secrecy might inhibit lawyers from asking all the necessary questions. Overall, Kunz said the client is being deprived of a lawyer's professionalism and legal skills if the code were to permit lawyers to reveal information that would help someone be exonerated.

Kunz added, "I think it's impossible to meet all the difficulties, it's impossible to solve." We don't agree, and urge the powers-to-be to make the effort. It may require some hard work, and it can be accomplished.

The Chicago Sun-Times also called for changes in the code after my exoneration. Expressing understanding and sympathy for the lawyers who remained silent in my case, the paper, nevertheless, called the code's secrecy provision an "abstract legal principle," concluding:

"This cannot be allowed to happen again. We support changes in the state's confidentiality rule."

I want to say a final word about Coventry and Kunz. Yes, I was angry at both of them when I first heard about the affidavit. Who wouldn't be? The two had a document that could have saved me from spending twenty-six years behind bars. However, as I learned about the code, I understood why Coventry and Kunz did what they did. As I have written, they abided by the rules. I know they took a lot of heat from the public. Should they have broken the rules? The ethics code notwithstanding, I would answer the question with a very strong, "Yes." That's the major point of writing this book.

I met Coventry and Kunz for the first time when I was invited to a speaking engagement at which they participated. I walked into the room, and the attorneys were standing on the other side. I recognized them from photos in the media. I approached them, and Coventry and Kunz took several steps backward. I stopped and laughed. Obviously, they would be concerned; they had no way of knowing what my reaction would be. I assured them I had no hard feelings toward them. Both expressed regret, and I responded, "It was water under the bridge." We never discussed the issue itself. Coventry and I met at several other speaking engagements; I saw Kunz only once after this first encounter.

My aunt, Barbara Cannon, told the media when I was exonerated that Coventry and Kunz did what they had to do. Nevertheless, she didn't forgive them completely. She met Kunz and Coventry during a taping of a TV show, and asked them: "If Alton had died in prison and Wilson had lived, would you have come forward and told us that Alton was innocent?" After all, I did have a heart attack in prison in 2007. Coventry and Kunz didn't answer; they appeared to be tongue-tied.

She didn't let up, stating she couldn't understand how Coventry slept at night with the affidavit locked up in a strong-box under his bed. She believed they should have found some way to get the information out.

In interviews with reporters from *The Chicago Sun-Times*, Aunt Barbara probably said it best, stating: "We pray this will be eye-opening for the people who are holding evidence. Hopefully, it will spark the law to realize they need to do some changing."

I want to conclude by saying that as a society we need to assure that an innocent person never sits in prison for a crime he/she didn't commit. It is impossible to argue that it is moral and ethical to sacrifice the life of an innocent person to defend a guilty one. It just can't be done. Lawyers and judges can argue all they want about the complexity of the lawyer-client confidentiality relationship. There can be no debate about the fact that our laws and ethics codes should—must—guarantee that the kind of injustice I endured never happens to anyone else again—ever.

14.

Readjustment

Between April, when I was released on bond, and the final court appearance when all charges were dropped in September, I was worried that something might still happen that would send me back to prison. I watched what I was doing. I believed the "system" would continue to use anything and everything against me.

After the September hearing, I realized I was finally free. At the same, I wasn't free. Why? Because I was still dependent on others—my family to survive. The state didn't offer me any kind of job training, skills training, reentry training, or other help.

My mother was gone and so was my grandmother, two people whom I loved very much. I lost the best years of my life, years in which people build careers and raise families. I had neither. I tried hard to readjust to being free.

Of course, it felt a little weird to be free. For twenty-six years, someone gave me orders every minute of the day. They ordered me when to get out of bed, when to sleep, when to eat, when to wash, when to go to the bathroom, etc. As a free man, I could do what I wanted to do, when I wanted to do it, how I wanted to do what I wanted to do, and I could decide if I wanted to do it at all. If someone tried to tell me what to do, it upset me. I reminded them that I was a free man and the time when someone could make demands of me was over.

All this took a little time to get used to. Frankly, I never got rid of all the feelings and habits I formed from having been in prison for so long. I don't know if I ever will. Being in such an abusive environment leaves a lasting impact. I still keep the same watchful eye on my surroundings, even on family members, as I did in prison. I can't avoid being suspicious of everyone. I don't question anyone about their motives or actions, but I am, as I said, very watchful. All this notwithstanding, learning to readjust outside the prison walls was very welcome, and I am delighted that this experience didn't affect the relationship with my family.

Although I thoroughly enjoyed my freedom, there were difficulties. Most importantly, I couldn't find a job. I looked diligently. Any kind of work would do; I wasn't particular. Every place I applied, the owners of the respective businesses said they were hiring. After I filled out the applications, I heard nothing.

I had a twenty-six-year hole in my work record. My resume included all the skills I acquired in prison. I attached my certificate of innocence as well as newspaper stories about what happened to me. It didn't matter. No one would give me a job after hearing the story. I lost count of the number of interviews I had. I was hired only twice for short periods. I also worked for my church.

None of the businesses admitted that they didn't believe my story, but it was clear that they remained suspicious despite all the documents I showed them. I had no choice. I basically retired; I was only in my mid-fifties.

My schedule was something like this: I would get up in the morning, walk the streets, and visit old friends, although I had lost a few. I was suffering from depression, and I was drinking a lot.

Slowly, I worked my way out of it. I lived with my aunt for about six months before I moved in with Terry, whom I would marry in 2013. I met her at a Labor Day family reunion about a year before I went to prison. After I was convicted, I asked Terry's aunt whether I could write to Terry. We exchanged letters, and developed feelings for each other. She attended my court hearings, and was very supportive throughout my years in prison, visiting me frequently. She helped me immensely with my readjustment after my release.

We had two marriage ceremonies. The first was at City Hall on April 3, and the guests included family members and a few friends. The second was held on August 17 at Mt. Carmel Missionary Baptist Church. Besides our relatives and friends, that ceremony was attended by Winston, Erica Reddick, and several people from Winston's office, including Christine

Komperda and Noel Zupancic, who worked, respectively, as a paralegal and investigator.

I became active again in church and joined the choir at Mt. Carmel. I began singing in a church choir when I was about ten and continued until I was sixteen. I quit and got in trouble on the streets as I wrote at the beginning of the book. I went to prison between the ages of twenty-one and twenty-six for the robbery charge that I described, and when I was released, I went back to church but the murder conviction for the shooting at McDonald's cut short my efforts to rebuild my life. After my exoneration, the church became important to me again.

The experience I had will be with me forever. This is something you can't forget or put behind you. I still try to understand it. It is very hard because there is no understanding it.

Despite all of this, I had no anger except at the system that allowed this to happen.

I got psychological help from Catholic Charities of the Archdiocese of Chicago, a nonprofit organization. I attended sessions once a week for about six months, and it helped a lot. I received one-on-one counseling and also participated in group therapy. After I filed my suit against the city, Catholic Charities ended my program because the city issued a subpoena for the organization to testify against me. Catholic Charities didn't want to have any part in it. This was one way the city got back at me. I never received any help after that.

I did spend a lot of time talking to the Rev. Dr. Joseph B. Felker, Jr., the pastor of Mt. Carmel Missionary Baptist Church.

In 2009, I joined the Life After Innocence (LAI) program sponsored by the Loyola University Chicago School of Law. Founded by Laura A. Caldwell, a professor at the law school, LAI offers exonerees guidance, pro bono legal services, and support on all levels. Students and faculty work with exonerees to have records expunged, find housing, search for employment, obtain counseling, procure identification, teach computer and cell phone skills, obtain medical treatment, and work with money managers to deal with any state funds or civil verdicts received after release.

I was still in the program at the time I was working on this book with Berl, and I am extremely grateful for all the assistance LAI has provided me.

LAI also assisted me in having all my records relating to the McDonald's murder expunged from the public record.

Although I was exonerated and issued a certificate of innocence, I was worried that anyone researching my case would discover that I was convicted of murder. They might not follow up and learn what happened to me. For instance, if I were stopped for a traffic violation, the police officer checking his/her computer could discover the conviction and probably would not take time to read all the records that proved my innocence.

LAI was aware of this problem not just in my situation but for all exonerees and worked to have their records expunged. Kimberly Mills, LAI assistant director and a Loyola University Chicago School of Law faculty fellow, supervised Loyola law students to assist exonerees in obtaining criminal records relief. She assigned Bethany Dixon to help me in expunging my wrongful conviction.

Bethany researched my case and prepared the necessary document over a seven-month period. She filed the required petition on October 28, 2016. We received a notice from the Cook County Circuit Court that a hearing on my petition would be held on January 10, 2017.

I was very nervous about what might happen. Despite my exoneration and the fact that I was granted a certificate of innocence, my cynicism about and distrust of the system was as strong as ever. However, I recognized that expungement would be the ultimate closure of my case.

Mills and I sat outside the courtroom waiting for my case to be called. Bethany could not attend because of a conflict in her schedule. After about an hour, a court employee handed us some papers. Our request for expungement had been granted and signed by LeRoy K. Martin, Jr., the presiding judge of the Cook County Circuit Court criminal division. We did not have to argue the case.

Under the expungement order, various police authorities would remove my records from their files, the Circuit Court would delete my name from the public record, and my record is not available to anyone for background checks.

Now, it was all over. Finally! No one would ever be able to find any records that I had been convicted of murder. I did not have to worry about explaining what happened to anyone in the future. I was very happy, and I stared at the papers for a long time before we left the court building. I was very grateful to LAI, Kimberly Mills, and Bethany Dixon.

One of the nice things that happened to me resulted from the publicity about my case in Chicago. I mentioned to a reporter that I wanted to see a Chicago White Sox baseball game. Mary Jo Cain-Reis, a real estate agent, read the story and sent me four tickets. My aunt, Barbara Cannon, and I went to the game. Somehow the White Sox organization heard that I was coming to the game, and we were seated in a fancy suite.

Mary Jo was quoted in the paper as saying, "I was choked up. My heart broke for this guy. This is going to be my crusade now. I feel like he is owed something."

She and a few of her friends even formed a Friends of Alton Logan Club and raised a little money for me. They were very kind to me, and I invited Mary Jo to my wedding.

Obviously, there had been major changes in technology. I learned how to use a cell phone very quickly, and had no problems with GPS systems. The computer was another matter; it wasn't easy to learn how to use it.

One positive that remained constant in my life was my faith in God. That never changed, no matter how difficult the issues. I continued to pray, read the Bible, and go to church.

In interviews and in guest appearances as a speaker, I was often asked how I kept my belief in the Almighty. I answered that I maintained my faith because I believed God was good and just.

A frequent question, for instance, was, "Did you believe He had forsaken you?" My answer was, "At one time I did feel that way, but I came to realize that He hadn't forsaken me. I had forsaken Him." I believed that my prison sentence was His way of teaching me something. We need to trust that though God may be testing us, He never abandons us.

In 2010, I participated in a performance of *The Seven Last Words of Christ* by Franz Joseph Haydn at the Rockefeller Memorial Center on the campus of the University of Chicago. It was broadcast by WFMT Radio in Chicago. I was among nine people, including then-President Obama, and seven distinguished world-renowned theologians, who read passages during the performance. It was a very moving event, one that I will never forget. In my part, I read about "abandonment," abandonment by family, friends, and politicians, and added that we also suffer from:

"Abandonment by some in our justice system who talk righteously about civil liberties but then, knowingly, allow the most inhumane injustices to occur."

I, unfortunately, had firsthand experience with that. I hope that the innocent who are locked up behind bars don't blame God—I didn't blame God—and that they keep their faith and never lose hope.

I was twenty-eight when I was arrested, fifty-five when released and exonerated, and sixty-four when we completed this book. I hope to live a long life with my family and my wife, Terry. I thought it would be appropriate to include a beautiful poem that Terry wrote and sent to me while I was in prison. I read it many, many times.

EVERLASTING

I am your earth, your sky and everything
your eyes see existing between the two;

I am your rainbow that shines after a
summer's rain when you feel sick or blue.

I am your companion or right side when you
feel isolated or alone;

I am your best friend there listening when
you need a shoulder to depend on.

I am your backbone—your inner strength
and pride to be the best you can be;

I am your answer to love and your commitment
to accept the responsibility is the key.

I am your heart's desire, your reflection of love's
glow that smiles on your face;

I am your sweet surrender surrounded by
the passion of your loving embrace.

I will pray that the innocent who are imprisoned will hear the steel doors of their cells unlock, and will walk out with their heads held high, even if it takes twenty-six years, as it did in my case.

15.

Addendum

So, how did the prosecutors who successfully had me convicted for a crime I did not commit feel about my exoneration? We contacted nine who worked on my case through the years, and what follows are the results of those calls.

- Richard M. Daley, state's attorney who prosecuted the case for about twenty years before it was turned over to the Attorney General's Office, did not return voice mail messages.[48]
- J. Scott Arthur, assistant state's attorney, still believed I was guilty. He thought the three witnesses were credible, and added he didn't believe the Kunz-Coventry story. When Berl pointed out that I was

---

48. At the time we tried to contact him in 2016, Daley was of counsel for the law firm Katten Muchin Rosenman LLP.

finally declared innocent, he responded with, "So they say. So they say."[49]

- Raymond P. Garza, assistant state's attorney, said he couldn't answer questions because the case was more than thirty years old, and he would have to review the files. He also said he would want to know more about what he called the "tenor" of our book before he participated in an interview. Berl responded that he respected that view and ended the conversation cordially.[50]

A few hours later, Garza called Berl, stating he had some questions and wanted to tape record the conversation. Berl said he had no objection. Garza became very combative, challenging every fact cited in the conversation. Berl had a hard time saying anything. Irate, Garza focused on Edgar Hope and had most of his facts wrong. He never mentioned Andrew Wilson, who killed Wickliffe. Berl gave Garza a brief outline of the book's contents, particularly as it related to the lawyer-client confidentiality part of the story. Garza's anger grew more intense when Berl refused to discuss what we wrote about prosecutors and police. He

---

49. In April 2001, Winston, pursuing the issue of missing police files, deposed Garza and in May 2001, he deposed Arthur. In the two depositions, Winston asked each of them about 150 questions related to my case. For more than 100 of those questions—about one third—the two responded either that they didn't know the answer, or they couldn't recall the respective information, whether it dealt with witnesses, the name of the lead detective on my case, if they talked to Burge regarding details about the murder, or whether they received any information that I wasn't the shooter.

50. See Note #49 above.

accused us of writing a trashy book and hung up the phone. The call confused Berl; he couldn't figure out why Garza had called.

- Vincenzo Chimera, of the Illinois Attorney General's Office, who joined the Cook County (Illinois) Circuit bench, returned a voice message. He said he needed to get approval to speak to us. He didn't say from whom. Judge Chimera never called back.

- Virginia Bigane, assistant state's attorney, called Berl twice after he left a voice message. She said she would be pleased to answer any questions after she reviewed her notes. He never heard from her again.

We left voice mail messages for, but did not receive any responses from:

- Richard D. Schwind, an assistant Illinois attorney general who became a Cook County (Illinois) Circuit Court associate judge.

- Ellen Mandeltort, assistant state's attorney, who also became a Cook County (Illinois) Circuit Court associate judge.

- Earl B. Grinbarg, an assistant state's attorney.

Berl also contacted the press office for Illinois Attorney General Lisa Madigan, who handled the case for about six years before dropping all charges against me in Judge Schreier's courtroom on September 4, 2008. Berl asked to speak to Attorney General Madigan. A few days after he made his request, a press spokesperson called him, stating while the Attorney General's Office was prepared to assist with documents, Attorney General Madigan wouldn't participate in an interview.

We had lots of questions for the prosecutors. For instance:

- How would they explain that the shell found at McDonald's was matched, six days after my arrest, to the shotgun discovered in Wilson's living quarters at his aunt's beauty shop?
- Or, what about the fact that Wilson had Wickliffe's revolver, which he stole from Wickliffe after shooting him, when Wilson was arrested?
- Or, why, as Wilson stated in his affidavit, didn't detectives ever interrogate him about the McDonald's murder?
- Or, what about all the missing police files?
- Or, why did they ignore the long partnership that Hope and Wilson had in committing crimes?
- Or, why didn't they interview witnesses who said I wasn't in McDonald's the night of the shooting?
- Or, what about the statements made by Donald White, who said that Hope and Wilson came to his house after the shooting and bragged about the murder, and showed off the guns Hope and Wilson had stolen?

These were just a few of the questions we would have liked to have them answer. I also wondered if the prosecutors heard "on the street" that an affidavit or some other kind of legal document existed that proved my innocence. It is a fair question since my lawyers heard those "rumors."

We had many other questions, including, most important: Were prosecutors unaware of all the misconduct committed by police that we cited in our lawsuit? They had to know, as I wrote at the beginning of my story, about many, if not all, of the abuses. They just turned a complicit blind eye to improve their conviction record.

(Incidentally, we tried to reach Alvin Thompson, the Cook County sheriff's deputy who was wounded in the McDonald's shooting, and one of the three witnesses who identified me as the one who shot and killed his partner, Lloyd Wickliffe. After an extended search, Berl located him in May 2017 at Prairie State College in Chicago Heights [thirty miles south of the Chicago Loop], where he was employed as a sergeant in the college's police department. But Thompson did not return Berl's phone messages. As to the other two witnesses, Charles Trent died before my second trial, and given her false testimony at my two trials, we did not try to find Anthonette Dawson.)

We would never get answers to any of our questions. Frankly, neither of us expected we would.

Yet, despite all I had learned about the so-called justice system—and while I didn't expect any remorse—I have to admit I remained disappointed at the lack of contrition. No one said, "We regret what happened," or "We made a mistake," or "We're sorry."

I would have liked to have heard those words. I don't think that was too much to ask for.

A word from Berl Falbaum on how this book came about...

I learned about Alton's case from the 2008 *60 Minutes* segment. The case was intriguing because of the ethical, moral, and intellectual issues it presented. I was working on another book at the time, so I placed a note in my files that when I finished the ongoing project, I might pursue his story. And, I did.

Alton lived in Chicago, while my home was in West Bloomfield, Michigan, about twenty-five miles northwest of Detroit. I tracked him down by phone and scheduled a "get acquainted" lunch in Chicago. At the lunch with Alton and his wife, Terry, I explained that I wanted to write a book on his story, and outlined the issues involved in such an undertaking. We talked for about two hours, and Alton said he would think it over.

About a week later, he sent me an email stating that he wanted to pursue the project. For several months, I frequently commuted to Chicago to interview Alton and conduct research in the offices of lawyers who represented him, the Cook County Public Defender's Office, and the Cook County Clerk's Office. In addition, I interviewed Alton by telephone many times.

I expected to work with a man who was bitter, angry, cynical, and, perhaps, depressed. That would certainly have been understandable and justified under the circumstances. To my amazement, I found a soft-spoken, sensitive human being with a delightful sense of humor. He criticized no one. No, that is not exactly accurate. During many hours of interviews, he only bristled—actually more than bristled—at the mention of Richard M. Daley, who, as Cook County state's attorney at the time, was in charge of his case. Daley not only persisted in prosecuting Alton, but also asked for the death penalty.

When I asked him about Daley, he exploded briefly, stating, "Don't mention that fucking name to me." He also was angry at the system generally.

If he was embittered at anything else, he certainly hid it well. Overall, he seemed to be a man at peace with himself. He did not ask the question that is almost a cliché, "Why me?" and did not engage in any, "What ifs?" He explained, "You can't live with the kind of situation I experienced and ask, 'What if?'" He accepted his fate without complaint and did not abandon his belief in God. Like other exonerees whose stories I had read, he did not want any revenge.

Some exonorees even offered "forgiveness." I have never understood their passiveness, or their disinterest in "getting even, getting their pound of flesh" after enduring what I consider the unendurable. I know I would not be that magnanimous if I suffered the injustice experienced by Alton and others wrongly convicted.

Alton's relatives whom I interviewed all said that whenever they saw him in court or visited him in prison, he was always jovial and in good humor, never displaying any depression, anger or bitterness. They were as mystified by his upbeat temperament as I was.

Nor did he express any hard feelings for the lawyers who remained silent about his innocence. He repeated many times that he could not blame them for "doing their job."

Alton responded to every question I asked; he ducked none. Generally, he gave brief answers because he is a man of few words. There were times, I sensed, that he did not want to talk about painful issues, especially his years in prison. Once, when I touched on a very sensitive point, he smiled slyly, looked me in the eye and said, "Berl, I'm going to choke you."

Alton surprised me constantly as we worked together. One experience that I will never forget was how he answered when I asked him to describe his feelings on being set free. He took a deep breath and exhaled with a long, "Ooooooooooooooooo."

I recognized the relief, sorrow, and pain embodied in that exclamation. He repeated the sound as if to emphasize his point and make sure I understood. He did not have to worry. I understood perfectly.

Even after being immersed in this book with Alton for

more than two years and editing and refining the copy many times, I still had a hard time coming to grips with what happened to him. I always felt anger and sadness that this could happen to anyone. The story never became mundane. There simply is no justification that excuses letting innocent people rot in jail.

To say that Alton is unique in light of the pain and suffering he experienced is, of course, an understatement. Periodically, when I interviewed him, one of his friends, Vencent Morris, would join us. I heard many "wows" from Morris as he heard Alton's answers to my questions. As tragic as Alton's experience was, it was stimulating to work with him and examine the ethical code relating to lawyer-client confidentiality. Our hope is that the legal community will review the issue and adopt reforms. I value the relationship I established with Alton, and I am grateful that he crossed my path.

Berl and I are reviewing draft copy of our book.

About the Co-Author

Berl Falbaum was a general assignment and political reporter for *The Detroit News* for ten years, administrative aide to Michigan's lieutenant governor for four years, and a PR executive in corporate public relations for fifteen years. For more than twenty-five years, he operated his own PR company, Falbaum & Associates. He has published eight other books and written one play, which was produced by a community theater. His articles on politics and the media appear frequently on the op-ed pages of Michigan's newspapers. He was an adjunct faculty member, teaching journalism, at Wayne State University in Detroit for forty-five years.

Acknowledgments

This section is usually reserved exclusively for an expression of gratitude to people who assisted in the development of a book, and we will thank those who helped us with ours.

First, however, I need to express my heartfelt gratitude to the lawyers who gave me back my life. They were totally committed and worked tirelessly to prove my innocence, overcoming every roadblock, and there were many. They fought the system, a system that has defeated many, and won victories no one could've expected. I wouldn't be writing this if it weren't for the selfless dedication and stubborn commitment of the lawyers who wouldn't settle for any result other than overturning my conviction.

So, thank you Harold J. Winston, assistant public defender and attorney supervisor in the Cook County Public Defender's office; assistant public defenders Erica L. Reddick who would join the Cook County Circuit Court bench, Brendan P. Max, and Susan Smith; Barbara C. Kamm, assistant appellate defender; Noel Zupancic, an investigator in the Public Defender's Office; Christine Komperda, a paralegal; and Elizabeth Turillo, a DePaul University College of Law student who helped on the case. I will always be grateful to all of you.

My thanks also to Jon Loevy, Russell Ainsworth, and Elliot Slosar, of the law firm Loevy & Loevy, for their fine work in winning the settlement that gave me financial security, security I needed desperately since I faced severe difficulties in reestablishing my life after my release.

I also want to express my appreciation to Jack P. Rimland, my attorney in the first trial; and Steve M. Wagner, who became a Cook County Circuit Court associate judge, and James A. Sorensen, my attorneys in the second trial. The verdicts notwithstanding, the three worked diligently on my behalf.

A special thank you to Laura A. Caldwell, a law professor at Loyola University Chicago School of Law, and founder of Life After Innocence (LAI), which does outstanding work in helping exonerees. LAI was instrumental in helping me get back on my feet. Indeed, at the time I wrote this book with Berl, some eight years after my exoneration, I was still receiving assistance.

Now to the book.

There are several people Berl and I need to thank for helping us with this project. We want to express our special gratitude, again, to Harold Winston. He explained complex legal issues and provided excellent counsel. We spent many hours in his office interviewing him and researching his files. He was always patient, never showing any frustration when faced with some very basic, layman's questions. We are not overstating it when we observe that this book wouldn't have happened without him.

Others we would like to acknowledge and thank (in alphabetical order) are:

- Russell Ainsworth, of the law firm, Loevy & Loevy.
- John T. Biga, chief deputy Cook County clerk, criminal division.
- Kenneth S. Broun, retired University of North Carolina School of Law professor.
- Bethany Dixon, Loyola University Chicago School of Law student.
- Barbara C. Kamm, assistant appellate defender.
- Jon Loevy, of the law firm Loevy & Loevy.
- Kimberly Mills, assistant director, Life After Innocence, and Loyola University Chicago School of Law faculty fellow.
- Mary Pollard of Prisoner Legal Services.
- Jack P. Rimland, attorney in my first trial.
- Richard Rosen, retired University of North Carolina School of Law professor.
- Patrick T. Santos, a California attorney.
- Elliot Slosar, of the law firm Loevy & Loevy.
- Estlin Usher, WFMT Radio Network, station relations manager.

- Paul Walton, Oakland County (Michigan) chief assistant prosecutor.
- Michael D. Warren, Jr., Oakland County (Michigan) Circuit Court judge.
- Marvin Zalman, professor of criminal justice at Wayne State University in Detroit.

We were saddened by the death of William Jameson "Jamie" Kunz in November 2016. While we disagreed with his decision to remain silent, we were impressed by his commitment to the legal code, and that he agreed to be interviewed for this book.

Similarly, we appreciated that Dale E. Coventry and Andrea D. Lyon talked to us extensively about their decision. They showed the courage of their convictions, which is more than many others did in this case.

We are also very grateful to Jack Shoemaker for lending his exceptional name in the publishing industry and that of Counterpoint Press to this project, and a thankful shout-out to his team—Jennifer Alton, Megan Fishmann, Jenn Kovitz, Shannon Price, Alisha Gorder, Wah-Ming Chang, Kelli Trapnell, and Irene Barnard—for their invaluable contributions. A special thank you to Bill Smith for his cover design. The powerful symbolism vividly captures the essence of my ordeal.

Many, many thanks to G. Flint Taylor, Maurice Possley, and Rob Warden for their kind and gracious words on the back cover.

To write this book, we researched court documents covering more than two and a half decades.[51] We examined news reports, and conducted interviews with many principals involved in the case. Regarding the media, after *60 Minutes* aired my story on March 9, 2008, coverage increased dramatically, and we used facts and quotes from news outlets, including but not limited to: *ABC Eyewitness News*, the Associated Press (AP), CBS's *60 Minutes*, Chicago Public Radio Station WBEZ, *The Chicago Reader*, *The Chicago Sun-Times*, *The Chicago Tribune*, and *The New York Times*.

Additional Acknowledgments from Berl Falbaum

I want to express my gratitude to:

Jack Koblin, a retired Chrysler Corporation attorney. He is a much-valued friend who reviewed the manuscript and offered many important suggestions.

Debbie Zager, my sister-in-law, for her keen eye in proofreading the manuscript. She made important contributions to three of my other books, and I am indebted to her once again.

I also received exceptional advice from Maury Kelman,

---

51. Unfortunately, most of the records in the Cook County clerk's office relating to Alton's case were lost. John Biga, chief deputy Cook County clerk, criminal division, searched diligently for weeks to locate legal filings, briefs, transcripts, court orders/decisions, and other documents, but to no avail.

who taught constitutional law for almost thirty years at Detroit's Wayne State University. Maury, who helped me on other books as well, was a close friend for forty-five years and he died in 2016 while I was working on this book. He was brilliant, and I miss him immensely.

My "landlady." My wonderful, loving niece, Emily Goldsmith, who put me up in her apartment in Oak Park, Illinois on my frequent visits to Chicago. Coincidentally, at the time, she worked as a Cook County assistant public defender. Staying in her apartment saved me the expense of a hotel, and gave me time to build on a valuable relationship that is very important to me.

Finally, my wife, Phyllis, who reads and edits all my work. She has always improved my writing as she has my life.

Index

Page references for illustrations appear in italics.